THE CHRISTIAN AND TECHNOLOGY

JOHN V FESKO

EP Books (Evangelical Press), Registered Office: 140 Coniscliffe Road, Darlington, Co Durham DL3 7RT

admin@epbooks.org

www.epbooks.org

EP Books are distributed in the USA by:

JPL Books, 3883 Linden Ave. S.E., Wyoming, MI 49548

order@jplbooks.com

www.jplbooks.com

British Library Cataloguing in Publication Data available

Print ISBN 978-1-78397-272-2

eBook ISBN 978-1-78397-273-9

Contents

Dedicated to the love of my life, Anneke Carmen

Preface

Technology is an ever-growing facet of our lives, and so, I have spent the last few years trying to keep up with the latest trends and developments. On the one hand, I am an avid user of technology. My smartphone is probably the most useful device I have ever owned. Not only is it my lifeline to my wife and family, but my phone also functions as my pocket-sized library and classroom. On the other hand, my research has taught me that technology is a double-edged sword that requires cautious and intentional use.

When my former colleague at Westminster Seminary California, Julius Kim, asked me to do a semester-long chapel series on a topic of my choice, I immediately thought of collating all of my research and reading into a small devotional book that would serve as the basis for my chapel addresses. I enjoyed writing this book and hope it proves useful and edifying for the church. Some of my greatest fears are based on the uncritical use of technology, that we will erode our capacity for God's word, become more self-centered, and turn our useful devices into idols. If I were to visually present my fears, perhaps Apple's 1984 Super Bowl advertisement that unveiled the Macintosh computer would aptly paint the picture. People sat entranced in front of a massive screen — a scene deliberately evocative of a dystopian Orwellian future — until a woman ran into the arena and threw a massive sledge hammer and shattered it. I do not bring a hammer to destroy technology; I am not a Luddite by any stretch of the imagination. Ease, entertainment, and convenience are not always godly pursuits. At the same time, I hope and pray that each of these devotional thoughts will cause us to carefully evaluate how we think about and use technology.

I am grateful to a number of people who have helped me see this book to publication: to my colleague, Julius Kim, for giving me the opportunity to deliver the series of chapel addresses; to the students who attentively listened and gave me helpful feedback;

and to my brother, Lee Eric Fesko, who read a draft of the manuscript and provided me with some good comments. Thank you to my mother-in-law, Linda Jones, for reading through the manuscript and giving me good feedback. And thank you to Graham Hind and the whole team at Evangelical Press. I am also grateful to my children, Val, Rob, and Carmen Penelope, for all of the love you give to me. Above all others, you are the three people in the whole world that I want to take this book to heart and pass it on to your children.

I am most thankful to my wife, Anneke, who listened attentively when I read draft chapters and then attended chapel to hear me deliver the devotionals. Thank you, Wife, for your love and interest in my work. You are my beloved wife, best friend, mother of our children, and love of my life. Therefore, I dedicate this book to you, Anneke Carmen.

Introduction

The bright white light of our smart phones is often the first thing to greet us in the morning. We wake up bleary-eyed in our darkened bedrooms. The sunlight has yet to pierce into the room. We reach for our phones and begin consuming data. We scroll through tweets, e-mails, news, and various social media outlets. In addition to this flurry of information, many people undoubtedly open their Bible apps and begin their day in prayer and Scripture reading. The use of our smart phones extends far beyond our devotional lives. I know of pastors who deliberately avoid saying, "Open your Bibles," from the pulpit on Sundays because they do not want to alienate those without a physical copy of God's word. Instead, they say, "Open your copy of

God's word," so that people with Bible apps do not feel ignored. Where physical copies of the Bible used to dominate, smart phones, iPads, and e-readers are quickly gaining ground and look like they might soon surpass Bibles. On the one hand, should it really matter what type of Bible you bring to church as long as you bring one? Moreover, why carry a bulky physical copy of the Bible when you can download a relatively inexpensive or even free Bible app? The app, after all, lets you carry a large Bible wherever you carry your phone, perform word searches in split seconds, highlight and bookmark key passages, record notes, and for more advanced apps, look-up words in the original Greek and Hebrew. Surely all of these benefits outweigh any of the potential drawbacks to using the Bible app on your smart phone?

On the other hand, we should ask, how is our use of technology shaping the way we live and think, and what is the impact upon us as we live the Christian life? Research shows how addictive smart phones can be, and how reading on screens is detrimental to your physical well-being. There are educational, physical, and mental drawbacks to using your smart phone: people who read physical copies of books have better long-term retention rates; physical books do not cause macular degeneration with prolonged use the way the blue-light emitting smart phones do; and reading on your smart phone screen re-wires your brain in such a manner as to affect your attention span negatively. There are benefits and drawbacks to this wonderfully useful and amazing invention. But what if I told you that the same pattern unfolds with every technological invention. For every two steps forward, we might actually take three steps backwards. We grow in our abilities in some areas with new technological advances and become weaker in other areas. If this pattern clearly emerges with smart phones, what other technological advances have shaped the way we live, both positively and negatively, and how have they impacted our Christian lives?

This small book reflects upon six different technological advances and considers how they have positively and negatively shaped our lives. How have screens, social media, the automobile, the book, virtual reality, and unfettered access to the world through the internet changed the way we live? How have they have the benefited and hindered our growth in grace? The apostle Paul exhorts us not to conformed to the patterns of this world but to be transformed by the renewing of our minds (Rom. 12:2). Many believe that technology is morally neutral and has no inherent negative effects on us, let alone on the quality of our spiritual lives. Conversely, there are certainly benefits to using technology but we must always beware of the drawbacks so that we profitably use the technology rather than allowing the technology to use us. In other words, we need not retreat into an enclave that shuns all forms of technology but neither should we use it uncritically. This book presents food for thought on how critically to use technology so we are aware of both its benefits and dangers lest we adversely affect our physical and spiritual lives.

Plan for the Book

In order to help people think through the implications of the various ways technology has impacted the church and to foster discernment, I present reflections on six different technologies. In the first chapter, I discuss screens — they are all around us: computer screens, phone screens, tablet screens, tv screens, jumbotron screens. Technology experts predict that they will only continue to spread. This chapter therefore asks the question: Have we become addicted to our screens? Should we allow something else other than God captivate our hearts? We have to ask the question: Are we using our screens or are our screens using us?

The second chapter discusses social media and its influence upon the church. Social media is not simply a digital meeting place for interaction with friends and family. Rather, it is a digital bazaar where companies want you to click on their advertisements and gaze at their websites. Social media is a money-making platform and the only way to generate cash-flow is to get users to click on links. News media outlets, therefore, will promote a cash-making agenda, which does not always reflect reality. News outlets also promote their own agendas. If this is the case then, we should ask ourselves: Who sets the agenda for the church? Are we meeting the needs of the church and our local communities or are we imposing someone else's agenda? Again, are we using social media or is social media using us?

The third chapter examines a technology that most of us likely take for granted, namely, the automobile. While we probably do not give our cars too much thought, it is one technological development that has radically changed the church. People used to go to church in their local community but now they can go wherever they want. Just because we can drive away from one church to another does not mean that we should. Has the automobile changed us from church members to church consumers? Are we members of a church that seek to serve and worship or customers who want to ensure we have a good experience?

The fourth chapter explores another ignored technological development in the book. Have we considered that inexpensive mass-produced books have only existed for the last five hundred years? How has the invention of the book changed the way we read and use Scripture? Correlatively, how have e-books changed the way we read our Bibles? There are undoubtedly many benefits to books and e-books, but we should not use them uncritically. This chapter challenges us not to allow books to keep us from memorizing Scripture because we now own a copy of the Bible. It also challenges us to recognize that the Bible is not a form of entertainment. Should we read our e-Bibles on the same screen where we watch movies, tweet, text, and surf the internet? Can we set aside those distractions and create sacred space so we can lose ourselves in God's word? This chapter asks and answers these important questions.

Chapter five investigates the benefits and dangers

of virtual reality. On the one hand, there are great benefits. Doctors can perform surgeries from a great distance where patients cannot access quality healthcare. Pilots can train in simulators without endangering lives. But to what extent should we use virtual or augmented reality if it displaces the good creation that God has given us? If virtual reality allows us to create a world tailor-made to our own liking, will the real world appear broken because it does not meet our expectations? Virtual reality technology can be fun, entertaining, and beneficial, but we must beware that we do not allow ourselves to create our own world that becomes an idol which displaces God's good creation.

The sixth and final chapter delves into the amazing access that technology like the internet gives us: We can buy all sorts of things with the click of a mouse; Google has scanned a fifth of the world's published books, which gives us unprecedented access to books, and we can purchase all sorts of services. But we also now have unconstrained access to evil and wickedness such as pornography and death as a form of entertainment. Pornography and death have slick websites and advertising and thus take on mundane forms, but the thin marketing veneer covers wickedness and even the demonic. Seeing that this evil is only a few mouse-clicks away, how do we handle our new unrestricted access to it?

Conclusion

In the end, we need not flee from technology but we must understand it in order to use it well. One of the primary themes of this book is encouraging us to look past technology and dig into our own hearts. It encourages us to ask whether Christ so fills us that nothing else can drag us away from him. Have you turned your screen into an idol? Have you allowed social media to become the rose-colored glasses through which you see the world? Have you allowed your automobile to flee from a church when you should stay? Does the fact that you own a copy of the Bible discourage you from memorizing God's word? Does God's beautiful creation seem broken in comparison with the virtual world that you have created? Does your unfettered access to all sorts of things through the internet encourage you to look at, read, and watch things that do harm to your soul? All of these questions represent the need to make Christ our chief priority in our lives. In the words of the old hymn:

> *Be Thou my Vision, O Lord of my heart*
> *Naught be all else to me, save that Thou art*
> *Thou my best Thought, by day or by night*
> *Waking or sleeping, Thy presence my light.*

When Christ fills our vision, we will be able to use technology aright — we will not allow it to lead us into temptation and will be savvy to the tendencies towards idolatry and spiritual sloth that accompany it. When we feed upon Christ, the manna from heaven, all else pales in comparison. We find satisfaction in the Lord and seek no other table at which to feed our hungry souls: Blessed are those who hunger and thirst for righteousness, for they shall be satisfied (Matthew 5:6).

ONE

Screens: The New American Idol?

IN THE ANCIENT BIBLICAL WORLD, idolatry was easily identified — look for a person bowing down to a block of stone or gold and you could observe idolatry in action. God commanded Israel that he alone was God and, therefore, to worship anything else was called idolatry (Exodus 20:3). Fast forward several thousand years and we can still find these easily identifiable forms of idolatry. I have peered into Buddhist temples in Asia and observed people bowing down and worshipping elaborate statues. In Western culture, whilst idolatry exists, discerning it can be more challenging because it looks like ordinary activity. This is where technology and screens enter the picture. All you have to do is walk through an airport terminal or down a busy city sidewalk and you can observe scores of zombie-like people walking with their heads down as they peer at their phones. They are scrolling through tweets, listening to music, or trying to search for something on the Internet. The use of screens is a common everyday occurrence, but not everyone who uses one automatically engages in idolatry. However, among those using screens, a large percentage of them are engaging in idolatry. While some might object to this generalization, the fact that books such as *The Digital Detox Plan* have now appeared indicates that a large segment of the population are increasingly addicted to their screens.

The Digital Detox Plan proposes twelve different signs that might indicate you're addicted to your screen. Ponder the following questions:

1. Do you check your phone first thing after you wake up, or check it in the middle of the night?
2. Do you slip away when you're with a group of people in order to check your phone?
3. Do you check your phone while you're eating with friends?

4. Have you ever bumped into someone because you're looking at your phone?
5. How much time do you spend outside away from your phone?
6. Is it difficult to complete a task without checking your phone?
7. Do you easily get distracted when you're offline doing other tasks?
8. Do you spend little face-to-face time with friends or family?
9. When you're home, is your family present but in different rooms interacting with separate screens?
10. Do you use a screen to pacify a child instead of talking, playing, singing, or reading to her?
11. Do you go online when you want to avoid an unpleasant task?
12. Have you tried to stop using your phone but have been unable to do so?[1]

To this list, I can add a few more questions. Have you ever:

1. Texted or surfed the internet during a church service?
2. Stepped out of a worship service to take a phone call? (If you are a brain surgeon, you can skip this question).
3. Decided to stay home and listen to a sermon online instead of go to church?
4. Binged watched TV shows on a regular basis or played video games into the early hours of the morning?

Any one of these things do not reveal that a person has turned their screen into an idol, but they are important questions to ask. We should not be afraid to look into the mirror of Scripture and ask whether our hearts have been captivated by something else other than God. If we think we might be bewitched by our screens, there are two possible paths. Either the world around us will change and we will inevitably use our screens less, or we have to be proactive about addressing our screen addiction.

Will Our World Change?

Might the world around us change where screens become irrelevant and therefore our screen time will naturally diminish? In other words, one of the keys to engaging addiction is to change your environment. Someone who struggles with alcoholism, for example, should avoid bars and liquor stores. So will our environment change? The answer to this question is, no. Our environment is unlikely to change. The more technology develops, the more screens will become ubiquitous. In his recent book, *The Inevitable: Understanding the 12 Technological Forces That Will Shape Our Future*, technology expert Kevin Kelly addresses the topic of *screening*.[2] That is, the idea that people will make more and more use of screens in their daily lives. At present, many people have smart phones, computers, smart watches, and tablets but screens will continue to spread.

Kelly offers a glimpse into the not-too-distant future where we will commonly find and use screens:

> *In the morning I begin my screening while still in bed. I check the screen on my wrist for the time, my wake-up alarm, and also to see what*

urgent news and weather scrolls by. I screen the tiny panel near the bed that shows messages from my friends. [. . .] I walk to the bathroom. I screen my new artworks [. . .] on the wall [. . .] I get dressed and screen my outfit in the closet [. . .] In the kitchen I screen full news. I like the display lying flat, horizontal on the table [. . .] I turn to the screens on my cabinets, searching for my favorite cereal [. . .] I dash to the car. In the car, my story continues where I left off in the kitchen. My car screens the story for me, reading it aloud as I ride. The buildings we pass along the highway are screens themselves [. . .] At my son's school, I check one of the public wall displays in the side hallway [. . .] I can also use the screen on my wrist [. . .] I finally make it to the office. When I touch my chair, my room knows me, and all the screens in the room and on the table are ready for me [. . .] After work I put on augmentation glasses while I jog outside [. . .] After our meal I will screen to relax. I'll put a VR headset on and explore a new alien city. [. . .] As I lay down, I set the screen on my wrist for 6am. For eight hours I stop screening.[3]

Kelly describes a world where screens are virtually everywhere: by our bedsides, on our wrists, in our bathrooms, in the kitchen, in the car, the hallways of buildings, in our offices, in eye glasses and VR headsets. It is difficult to think of a place where screens will not appear. Kelly describes this future world as an *inevitability*, the chief thesis of his book. In other words, the progress of technology will inevitably lead to the world that Kelly depicts.

Yet, the disturbing thing about Kelly's prophetic claim is how eerily similar it is to Ray Bradbury's dystopian novel, *Fahrenheit 451*.[4] Bradbury's novel famously describes a future where firemen no longer extinguish fires but rather start them. Firemen have the job of burning books because the government has outlawed them. Bradbury wrote the book in the vein of George Orwell's *1984* (1949) and Aldous Huxley's *Brave New World* (1932). But what makes Bradbury's vision of the future so relevant is that he predicted the widespread use of screens in the 1950s when he first wrote his novel. Television was a budding technology yet, long before the birth of the smart phone, Bradbury had the foresight to anticipate the spread and use of screens. In one disturbing scene, Bradbury writes about a woman who mindlessly overdoses on sleeping pills as she sits in her home staring at massive screens for hours upon end in her 'TV Parlor.' One of Bradbury's characters makes the following observation about the TV Parlor phenomenon:

> *You play God to it. But who has ever torn himself from the claw that encloses you when you drop a seed in a TV parlor? It grows you any shape it wishes! It is an environment as real as the world. It becomes and is the truth. Books can be beaten down with reason. But with all my knowledge and skepticism, I have never been able to argue with a one-hundred-piece symphony orchestra, full color, three dimensions, and being in and part of those incredible parlors.*[5]

In Bradbury's dystopian world, screens engulf, overwhelm, and anesthetize viewers so that they stop thinking and simply experience what is on the screen. Bradbury's fictional world looks very much like Kelly's anticipated future world of wall-to-wall screens. But in Bradbury's world, the proliferation of screens is a nightmare whereas in Kelly's mind, they are the next desirable and beneficial evolutionary technological phase. Therefore, what is it, nightmare or a dream come true?

There is too much evidence that points in the direction that the proliferation of screens is a nightmare. Significant research links the use of screens to depression, suicide, physical problems such as insomnia, macular degeneration, and attention deficit disorders.[6] A telling sign of the dangers of screens ironically comes from the chief architect of the iPad, Steve Jobs. When Jobs unveiled the iPad in 2010, he touted its virtues as to why this new screen was the best way to look at pictures, listen to music, or take classes on iTunes U. He thought that everyone should own an iPad. But in another context, Jobs admitted that his own children had never used one. Jobs told a New York times reporter, 'We limit how much technology our kids use in the home.'[7] This same reporter spent an evening with Jobs and his family and noted that no one pulled out a screen the whole evening. The reporter noted that the people producing screens and technology were following the drug dealer's cardinal rule: never use your own product.[8] All of this information should impress upon all screen users that they are not going away. They can be mind-numbing, medically harmful, and highly addictive so much so that their creators keep them at arm's length and away from their children. In light of this, what should a Christian do?

Proactive Remedies for our Idolatry

From one vantage point, our use of screens looks mundane — virtually everyone uses them, so what is the harm? On the other hand, screens are a hotbed of addiction, or what the Bible calls idolatry. That is, giving something or someone else the due attention reserved for God. We can all agree, therefore, that idolatry is wrong and we should not use our screens to promote sin. But how can we remedy our screen addiction? There are at least three potential paths. First, we can go cold turkey and eliminate the screens in our lives. We can throw out our cell phones, tablets, computers, and televisions. But in our ever hyper-connected world, is such a course of action possible? A second option is to follow a detox plan. There are apps that monitor and reduce your screen time. One author suggests making a sanctuary space, a place where you leave all technology at the door where you can meditate.[9] Or in his book *Hamlet's BlackBerry* (which now sounds very dated!), author William Powers and

his family disconnected their Internet connection one
day a week:

> *We called it the Internet Sabbath. 'Ye shall
> kindle no fire throughout your habitations
> upon the sabbath day,' says the Book of Exodus,
> and that's basically what we were doing with
> our screens. They might still be glowing, but
> without a connection they wouldn't be much of
> a draw.*[10]

These are both possible options, but Powers's
suggestion of an Internet Sabbath unintentionally taps
into an important biblical principle — worship.

The Sabbath was supposed to be a day of rest and
worship for Israel, a day in which they set aside all of
their lawful ordinary activities and labors so they
could devote the day to exercises of private and public
worship. God mandated this activity because we have
been designed to worship. We will worship something,
but the important question is, what or who? In other
words, we can go cold turkey or figure out a way to
manage our screen time, but we might never address
the underlying problem — our desire to worship
something other than God. We can throw out our

screens and still harbor idolatry in our hearts. We can manage our idolatry so we only engage in it for several hours a day, but this does not change the fact that we are still addicted to our screen. We are simply highly-functional screen addicts who manage our addiction. It does not change the fact that we are seeking contentment and satisfaction in something other than God. In his book that predicts the inevitability of technological trends, Kelly makes an unintentionally insightful claim: 'We keep on inventing new things that make new longings, new holes that must be filled.'[11] Kelly never stops to ask the question why humanity has an insatiable desire continually to invent or why we have holes in our lives that must be filled.

Early church theologian St. Augustine observed that all humans have a hole in their heart: 'You stir man to take pleasure in praising you, because you have made us for yourself, and our heart is restless until it rests in you.'[12] We have a God-shaped hole in our lives that only the Lord Jesus Christ can fill. We are aware of this hole and often desperately run to and fro seeking to fill it, and in this case, many of us try to fill it with our screens. But before we know it, we are addicted, and we end up engrossed with the luminous glow of our screens and God becomes a distant memory forgotten in the flurry of videos, pictures, hyperlinks, and apps that deluge our minds. Rather than coming to the table that God has prepared for us where he sets forth Christ, the manna from heaven, we come to the feast stuffed on what the world has to offer through our screens. We have engorged ourselves and therefore have little appetite for Christ.

Yet the Psalmist presents an entirely different picture when he writes: 'Oh, taste and see that the Lord is good! Blessed is the man who takes refuge in him' (Psalm 34:8)! The Psalmist's desire was for God, which he describes in terms of *tasting*, and in other Psalms *longing* and *thirsting*: 'As a deer pants for flowing streams, so pants my soul for you, O God. My soul thirsts for God, for the living God' (Psalm 42:1-2a). Unlike Kelly's unending cycle of trying to fill the void in our lives with newer and better technological innovations, Christ tells us that we find rest, peace, and satisfaction only in him: 'I am the bread of life; whoever comes to me shall not hunger, and whoever believes in me shall never thirst' (John 6:35). Only Christ can satisfy and only in him will we find peace.

Conclusion

When it comes to our screens, we must ask the piercing question: Are we using the screen or is the screen using us? Have we given ourselves over to an idol? In the end, we must realize that the screen is not the problem but rather our hearts are. We can address the symptom and reduce our screen-time and never scratch below the surface to the root cause: our restless idolatrous hearts. If we want to address our idolatrous addiction, we can use some of the advice mentioned above. We can limit our screen time, keep our phones at arm's length, put them in a different room at night, turn them off for set periods of time. However, if we fail to draw near to Christ through word, sacrament, and prayer, we will still long to fill the holes in our hearts. Only by feeding on Christ through his appointed means will we find peace and rest. Only then will we be able to use our screens rather than have them use us.

TWO

Social Media: Whose Agenda?

ONE RECENT TECHNOLOGICAL innovation is the invention of social media. The most popular platform is Facebook, a social media site that boasts millions of users. According to one recent source, one out of every three Americans is on Facebook every day. As of 2014, the site had 1.3 billion users worldwide. This means that at least one quarter of the earth's adult population has a Facebook account.[1] There are certainly many benefits to social media. You can stay in touch with friends and family even though they might live thousands of miles away. Churches maintain Facebook sites so that congregants can stay in touch and pass along information about upcoming church events. Many people also keep abreast with current events by staying connected with the Facebook pages of news media outlets. There are many good things about social media sites. But for every so-called advancement in technology, we might not realize that there can be correlative setbacks. C. S. Lewis once opined that each scientific advance and so-called 'conquest of nature' left humanity a little weaker as well as stronger: 'In every victory, besides being the general who triumphs, he is also the prisoner who follows the triumphal car.'[2] I think most people think of technological advances in terms of making forward progress — two steps forward. But with each technological development, the reality is that we make two steps forward and one, two, or maybe even three steps back. Therefore, if we make several steps forward with social media with all of its benefits, what is one of the backward steps that we unintentionally make?

If we regularly interact with people on social media, the consequence is that this becomes a source of our understanding of the world. It used to be that people watched the evening news to see what was going on in the world. In the 1960s, people watched the nightly news reports about the Vietnam War to understand what was going on in Southeast Asia. These nightly news reports caused many people to question and bring the war to an end. People looked at the world through their television screens but now people look at the world through the Internet, and one of the most common filters is social media sites like Facebook. What happens when pastors and elders view the world through Facebook and then shape their ministry and the church's agenda based on what they have seen and read? Is this a good or desirable way to shape a church's ministry? The short answer to this question is, no. Why? The answer lies in how social media sites like Facebook make money.

How Facebook Makes Money

In the Spring of 2018, Facebook CEO Mark Zuckerberg testified before the Senate in the wake of the Cambridge Analytica Scandal where 87 million Facebook users had their personal data used without their consent by a political firm to influence the 2016 elections.[3] At the hearing, one of the senators asked Zuckerberg how Facebook handles ex-user data, and Zuckerberg's response explained how the social media site generates capital from its users. Facebook does not sell its user's personal data to companies. Instead, Zuckerberg told the senators:

> *What we allow is for advertisers to tell us who they want to reach, and then we do the placement. So, if an advertiser comes to us and says, 'All right, I am a ski shop and I want to sell skis to women,' then we might have some sense, because people shared skiing-related content, or said they were interested in that, they shared whether they're a woman, and then we can show the ads to the right people without that data ever changing hands and going to the advertiser.*

In other words, when you upload information to Facebook about your opinions, activity, hobbies, vacations, preferences, political views, jokes, and search history, the website's software directs advertisements and web-content to your computer screen or phone based upon your inputted user-data. Ever since Facebook became a publicly traded company, this technological firm has been in the business of making money. Facebook may have started off as a website dedicated to connecting friends across the information highway but make no mistake, it is now a multi-billion dollar company. According to one source, in 2017, Facebook generated $39.9 billion of its

$40 billion profits from advertisements.[4] This means that the Facebook phenomenon is not what its users think it is. Scores of people undoubtedly use Facebook as a way to connect with people; they use it as a tool for social interaction. However, when you log onto the website, you have to realize that you are actually entering a virtual mall where clicking on links often constitutes making a purchase. Moreover, if Facebook matches your browsing experience with the nature of your inputted data, then you have to ask an important question: Have you truly looked at the world or only gazed into the mirror, a mirror created by the data generated by your clicks and pics? We should also connect this question to the related topic of news media and Facebook.

Whatever pretensions news media outlets have about providing insightful journalism, exposés on corrupt politicians, and news coverage about the latest world events, at the end of the day, they are in the business of making money. News media companies *sell* news. Through websites like Facebook, news is no longer strictly news but a means of generating revenue, and the most effective means of generating revenue is by being entertaining. Despite the fact that it was originally published in 1986, Neil Postman's

Amusing Ourselves to Death still offers a trenchant critique of the news entertainment business.[5] When Postman first wrote the book, the news media employed television, print, and radio. Whilst those mediums still exist, news media has since expanded into the Internet and social media sites like Facebook. Postman wrote of the melding of news and commercialism by exposing the insanity of a newscaster speaking about the dangers of nuclear holocaust where millions might be incinerated, which is then followed by commercials about hamburgers.[6] What does it mean when a newscaster spends thirty seconds reporting on a tragedy where hundreds of people were killed followed by a thirty-second advertisement about the new bacon double-cheeseburger?

While the medium has shifted from television to the Internet, think about the space on your Facebook page. As I scroll down my Facebook page, I see a post about social justice and the gospel followed immediately by an advertisement of equal size from a department store advertising children's shoes which is then flanked by two other advertisements: one for a grocer and another for a fitness-themed vacation. The same is true for major news media sites, such as

CNN.com, which has advertisements for a clothing company, a computer accessory, and a Bluetooth audio speaker. News media outlets want to deliver news, but they also want to generate revenue. And the only way they can deliver the news is if they generate money, and the only way they will generate money is if you click on their links and advertisements. Facebook does not generate $39.9 billion dollars of revenue by delivering what you need to read and view but rather what sells the most clicks.

This means that news media outlets and Facebook do not push information that you need to know but rather what sells based upon what you like to read and watch. Computer algorithms feed you content to filter through the ocean of information. But as Kevin Kelly notes in his book, *The Inevitable*, 'The danger of being rewarded with only what you already like, however, is that you can spin into an egotistical spiral, becoming blind to anything slightly different, even if you'd love it.'[7] In other words, you are not really looking at the world but rather into your own reflection in the Facebook mirror. What if you determine to read content that is 'trending,' even content that presents a different point of view? If trending news stories are generated by 'likes,' then you still cannot necessarily trust what you see on your screen. Christian Rudder documents the practice of buying Twitter followers. You can pay $20 and get 1,000 new followers. During the 2016 presidential race, New Gingrich boasted that he had six times as many Twitter followers as all of the other candidates combined. The problem was that he had paid for 90 % of them.[8] Therefore, what you might think is real, relevant, and pressing may only be an artificial digital campaign to push money-generating content. When it comes to picking Bible study topics, ideas for sermons and sermon series, teaching and sermon illustrations, or even topics of discussions with people in your church, what will you say? Will you base your decision on what you see on Facebook and the Internet? Will you use Facebook or will Facebook *use you* to sell more clicks to your friends?

How to Set the Agenda

Facebook and other social media sites are an unreliable window on the world; they are artificial environments that people build based on their personal interests and preferences. They are a digital bazaar where vendors shout from their stalls in order to sell you their wares. While a discerning user can filter through a lot of the noise, the best way to set the agenda for your church is through face-to-face interaction with the people in your church. The Bible has numerous examples of how to determine the needs of your church, but one of the most common ways appears in the church's regular gathering for corporate worship. Luke records that the early church devoted themselves to the apostles' teaching and 'the fellowship, to the breaking of bread and the prayers' (Acts 2:42). Luke also notes that members of the church 'were selling their possessions and belongings and distributing the proceeds to all, as any had need. And day by day, attending the temple together and breaking bread in their homes, they received their food with glad and generous hearts, praising God' (Acts 2:45-47). In other words, as they met together, they learned of one another's needs and sought to meet them through sacrificial giving. James counsels his recipients to 'confess your sins to one another and pray for one another' (James 5:16). In James's world, this meant having face-to-face conversations to learn of one another's needs so people in the church could lift one another up in prayer. Likewise, the apostle Paul exhorted the Colossians to teach and admonish one another in all wisdom, through the singing of psalms, hymns, and spiritual songs (Colossians 3:16). The Internet and social media like Facebook does not make these patterns of interaction irrelevant. In fact, it should cause us to be more and more devoted to them.

As you interact with the people in your church, you will learn of struggles, cares, concerns, loss, and heartaches. You will quickly determine what the people in your church need. Hashtags and likes should not drive your church's agenda, but rather interaction with the daily lives of your congregation. Only by spending time with the people will you discover their true needs. When you have fellowship over a shared meal, you will often find that people will open up and become vulnerable. Such times of vulnerability present opportunities for prayer and interceding on behalf of your brother or sister in Christ. In short, the Bible touts the importance of community, of the church, for setting the agenda in the church, not the digital marketplace of Facebook. Dietrich Bonhoeffer wrote about the balance that one must maintain between the individual and the community:

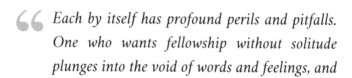

Each by itself has profound perils and pitfalls. One who wants fellowship without solitude plunges into the void of words and feelings, and

the one who seeks solitude without fellow̲
perishes in the abyss of vanity, self-infatuat̲
and despair.[9]

We are individuals. But we are also individuals that
have been united to the body — a group of people that
we both need and upon whom we depend. Only when
we are in close fellowship with them can we know
what is best for them. If we try to set the church's
agenda through concerns fed by social media and the
Internet, we run the risk of imposing a set of market-
driven personally shaped concerns on the church
rather than being sensitive to what the church truly
needs. In Bonhoeffer's words, 'The person who loves
their dream of community will destroy community, but
the person who loves those around them will create
community.'[10]

This brings us to a second point regarding setting
the church's agenda. As important as it is to know the
needs of the church through face-to-face interaction,
we must recognize who ultimately sets the agenda for
the church. As Bonhoeffer notes,

“ *God has already laid the only foundation of*
   our fellowship, because God has bound us

> *together in one body with other Christians in Jesus Christ, long before we entered into common life with them, we enter into that common life not as demanders but as thankful recipients.*[11]

The chief means by which God sets the agenda is through his word. 'God has put his Word into the mouth of men,' writes Bonhoeffer, 'in order that it may be communicated to other men.'[12] Protestants have historically recognized that God speaks to his people through the preaching of his word. Martin Luther once wrote of the Scriptures: 'Those words of God are not of Plato or Aristotle but God himself is speaking.'[13] Or, in the words of one sixteenth-century Protestant confession: 'Wherefore when this Word of God is now preached in the church by preachers lawfully called, we believe that the very Word of God is proclaimed, and receive by the faithful.'[14] Who better to set the church's agenda than God through his word?

In other words, if we set the church's agenda through our perusal of social media sites and the Internet, we will likely run into the problem of preaching, teaching, and discussing what our 'itching ears' want to hear (2 Timothy 4:3) — itching ears that have been piqued by advertisements, likes, and the effort to make money. If we realize, however, that the Bible is God's personal word to his people, then every time we read and hear it preached, God sets the agenda for his church and for our lives. Rather than hunting for Bible verses that support our opinions about the latest trending news story or bout of hashtag activism, what if God has something else in mind as we carefully read through his word or when ministers preach verse-by-verse and chapter-by-chapter through books of the Bible? Only when we cut God's word loose on the church will we find that the gospel of Christ will impact lives. Again, as Bonhoeffer observes, 'We must be ready to allow ourselves to be interrupted by God. God will be constantly crossing our paths and canceling our plans by sending us people with claims and petitions.'[15] In other words, when God sets the church's agenda, it might look different than our own or what happens to be trending on Facebook.

Conclusion

Will social media, hashtags, 'click ads', and our own web-surfing habits inform and form the church's agenda? My hope is, no. Social media has many benefits, but if we lose sight of what it is and how it functions, we can quickly misuse it and create chaos in the church. Early twentieth-century Presbyterian theologian J. Gresham Machen once observed the same type of disruptive patterns in the church long before the advent of the Internet and social media. He noted that when people sought the gospel of Christ and the word of God, they only found the turmoil of the world:

> *The preacher comes forward, not out of a secret place of meditation and power, not with the authority of God's Word permeating his message, not with human wisdom pushed far into the background by the glory of the Cross, but with human opinions about the social problems of the hour or easy solutions of the vast problem of sin. Such is the sermon.*

Machen laments, 'Thus the warfare of the world has entered even into the house of God.' He asks the pressing question,

> *Is there no refuge from strife? Is there no place of refreshing where a man can prepare for the*

battle of life? Is there no place where two or three can gather together in Jesus' name, to forget for the moment all those things that divide nation from nation [. . .] to forget human pride, to forget the passions of war, to forget the puzzling problems of industrial strife, and to unite in overflowing gratitude at the foot of the Cross?'

Machen concludes,

If there be such a place, then that is the house of God and that the gate of heaven. And from under the threshold of that house will go forth a river that will revive the weary world.[16]

In the end, use Facebook but ensure that Facebook does not use you.

THREE

The Automobile

WHEN WE THINK OF TECHNOLOGY, our minds likely
drift towards the latest gadget, smart phone, tablet, or
computer, but we might not give much thought to
common technological advancements that have
become relatively old, at least in comparison with
smart phones, for example. One such technological
advancement is the automobile. Compared to the
smart phone, which debuted with the launch of the
iPhone in 2007, a little more than a decade ago, the
automobile entered the American scene in the late
nineteenth century and thus has been a common
feature of our culture for more than one hundred
years. Most consider the automobile as mundane and
ordinary, but in the big picture of church history over

the last two thousand years, the automobile is a recent technological advancement that has dramatically reshaped and impacted the church. Some might only look at the positive aspects of the invention of the automobile but, as we noted in the last chapter, for every step forward there are two or three steps backward. In this case, the automobile has changed the church in significant ways and we need to be aware of how this technology has shaped the church so we can properly use our automobiles rather than allow them to twist and deform our relationship to the church.

The church before and after the automobile

In order to understand the effect of the car, we must briefly take a step back into the past in order to understand what church life was like before its advent. Prior to the mass production of the automobile, church life was quite different. In the Middle Ages, for example, most people in rural villages lived on the estate of a wealthy nobleman, and the lord of the estate had a church on his land for the local village. In some cases, estates were so vast that there were several villages and churches. But the vast majority of villages had one church, which people called a *parish*.[1] These churches were central features to community life and built out of stone.[2] Naturally, in cities, churches took on a grander scale due to the larger populations that lived around them; cathedrals sprung up around numerous European cities.[3] Regardless of whether one attended a village church or a city cathedral, both types of churches had one thing in common: church members lived within a walking distance. At maximum, if it was too far to walk, perhaps wealthier families had access to horse-drawn transportation.

There are several correlates of the placement and location of churches in the Middle Ages. Firstly, an entire church's membership lived within walking distance of their local church, within a few miles at most. Secondly, churches were therefore closely embedded in local communities. Thirdly, the proximity between the church and its members meant that they formed a close-knit community. In the sixteenth century, pastors and elders frequently visited the members of their congregations in order to pastor them and tend to their various needs.[4] Fourthly, there was a sense in which church members were held captive to their local church. There was only one local option and thus people, for better or for worse, had to attend the only church to which they had access. In larger cities, where there might be one or more churches in relative proximity, pastors were typically in close communication with one another so that if a wayward church member drifted to another congregation, the pastor could quickly address the situation. The automobile changed this picture in dramatic ways.

The automobile gave church members something they did not previously possess — mobility. From the earliest days of the church until the early part of the twentieth century, people either walked or rode their horses to church. They lived in close proximity to their local church. Or in some cases, some lived in rural areas where there was no church nearby, which meant that they did not attend church.[5] The automobile changed all of this. One periodical triumphantly proclaimed: 'The day of the horse is gone. The automobile has driven him from the roads. The boys and men and women of this generation must have automobiles.' The author touted the benefits of the car such as saving lives, preventing crime — all in order to 'keep up with the process of a moving world'.[6] Subsequently, churches adapted to the changing environment by purchasing land adjacent to their buildings in order to accommodate the sea of vehicles.[7]

Ministers and churches were eager to adopt the new technology for the sake of promoting the gospel. Pastors could now expand their reach to people living in remote areas. In some denominational contexts, multiple churches only needed one pastor since he could drive from church to church, preaching his message.[8] Churches also began to relocate near the burgeoning and ever-growing highway system.[9] In a very short period, local parishes quickly expanded beyond the idea of walking-distance which had marked the church for nearly two millennia.

But the introduction of the automobile was not a value-neutral technology. People saw all sorts of potential nestled in the automobile; they saw the ability to transform and industrialize rural America through rapid transportation which was now easily available. President Theodore Roosevelt introduced the Country Life Commission, which was tasked with transforming rural life to industrial standards.[10] In other words, capitalism and its thirst for ever-expanding markets found in the automobile the perfect instrument to implement its ideals and transform the American landscape — to make it more efficient and to create more consumers in order to feed the economic engine. A tell-tale sign of this development was the call for churches to pay their pastors better salaries so they could purchase automobiles. 'To 'buy a Ford' does not impoverish [ministers],' wrote one person, 'but increases their profitable efficiency.' Automobiles made farmers more efficient consumers and thus they should expect no less of their ministers.[11]

On the one hand, there are undoubtedly many benefits attached to the advent of the automobile. People in remote areas can now attend churches that are beyond walking distance. Conversely, ministers of the gospel can reach people in remote areas that were, for all intents and purposes, unreachable. If a church became liberal in its theology, a person was no longer stuck to the church in his local community but could now flee to a biblically-faithful church even if it was much farther away. Over the years, I have heard of people driving an hour or more to attend church because there is a dearth of biblically-faithful churches in their local communities. But what are the negative consequences of the introduction of the automobile to the life of the church?

Automobiles are not merely a means of traveling great distances in shorter periods of time or an inexpensive, quick, and efficient means of transportation. Rather, the invention of the automobile became a chief ingredient in capitalism and consumerism. If your local market did not carry the type or quality of product you desired, you could drive to a different market to find it. Such consumerism is not necessarily negative when you are looking for a better widget. The freedom to find the very best widget is certainly a great benefit. But is the church a widget? The same patterns of ever-expanding markets and automobile-driving consumers in search of a better widget has irreversibly altered the church, at least on this side of heaven. The automobile has transformed members of a local church imbedded in a village or city into consumers. If a pastor's message offends, attendees can look for a different church. If a local church does not meet their perceived needs, congregants can search for a church that does. If controversy embroils a church in acrimonious debate, people can leave for a more peaceful ecclesiastical setting. If a church tries to exercise discipline, the erring member can drive to another church in another community where no one is aware of his transgressions. Or, if a church does not meet your every theological requirement, you can drive the highways and byways until you find the perfect church.

In short, the automobile has transformed many church members into consumers.

Treating the church like a marriage

We cannot turn back the clock and return to a time when automobiles did not exist, even though some, like the Amish community, have done this very thing. All technological advancements call for wisdom when we consider the best way to employ them. We can and should celebrate the fact that cars have provided many blessings to the church such as accessibility for church members and an expansion of the church's reach to pastor those living in rural areas. But at the same time, just because we can drive away from one church and start attending another does not mean that we should. When we join the church, we explicitly vow to submit ourselves to the church's authority in our doctrinal beliefs and everyday practices. One Presbyterian denomination asks prospective members to affirm the following vow: 'Do you promise to participate faithfully in this church's worship and service, to submit in the Lord to its government, and to heed its discipline, even in case you should be found delinquent in doctrine or life?'[12] While this might wrinkle the noses of some, it merely reflects biblical teaching, such as when the author of Hebrews exhorts his readers: 'Obey your leaders and submit to them, for they are keeping watch over your souls, as those who will have to give an account. Let them do this with joy and not with groaning, for that would be of no advantage to you' (Hebrews 13:17). In this case, if your church determines that you have sinned and deem discipline as the necessary remedy, just because you can drive away does not mean that you should.

Similarly, factionalism has plagued the church since the earliest days. The apostle Paul rebuked the Corinthians for their party spirit because some claimed to follow Paul, others Apollos (1 Corinthians 3:4). The same can be said of the church at Rome, which had factions that did and did not eat meat (Romans 14:1-4). I suspect that if the Corinthians and the Romans had cars, each faction would have driven away and started the First Church of Corinth of the Paulinists or the First Church of Rome, Vegetable-Eaters Only. The churches at Rome and Corinth did not have this option so they had to follow Paul's counsel and recognize that he did not die for them and neither did Apollos but that they were all one body in Christ. Likewise, the meat-eaters and the vegetarians had to learn to love one another — the confident meat- eater had to learn to exercise loving patience towards his vegetarian brother, and conversely, the vegetarian had to cease his censoriousness against his meat-eating brother. In other words, just because we have a means of escape does not mean we should use it.

All too often, people in the church live like consumers rather than members. Consumers look for what suits them best rather than seek to love, sacrifice, and submit — to love their brothers and sisters, to sacrifice for them, and to submit to the authority of church leadership. Rather than consumers, we should try to view our membership as something closer to marriage. The biblical ideal has very few reasons why a married couple can seek divorce: sexual infidelity or abandonment (Matthew 4:31; 19:7-9; 1 Corinthians 7:11-12). Granted, church membership vows are not as strict. There are a number of reasons why someone might legitimately leave a church: physical relocation, a church's doctrinal infidelity, the church closes down, the pastor leaves and the church takes an inordinate amount of time to find a suitable replacement, or the church wrongly accuses you of doctrinal or moral sin. But at the same time, if we treat our membership vows more like marriage vows, then we might find that we have a more biblical relationship with our church.

When we find that our church develops doctrinal problems, we should stay, pray, and obey. We should not immediately run for the car but rather exercise patience towards our leaders, pray fervently on their behalf, and submit to their authority. If we find that our church becomes deficient in its outreach or programs, rather than run for the car, you can become the change you desire to see. You can volunteer to provide meals for those who are ill, or host the young people in your home, or teach Sunday School when no one else will. And even if church leadership makes a disagreeable decision, you nevertheless submit to their authority and echo the life of Christ in his humble submission to the authorities in his day. In the event that you find yourself placed under church discipline, as tempting as it might be to flee, remember that church leaders are God's instruments by which he exercises his loving, fatherly care for us: 'God is treating you as sons. For what son is there whom his father does not discipline' (Hebrews 12:8)? Your car may give you the ability to run away, but you might just be running from the very thing that you so desperately need.

Conclusion

Traditional marriage vows speak of loving your spouse 'from this day forward, for better, for worse, for richer, for poorer, in sickness and health, until death do us part.' While we have greater freedom with respect to our church membership vows, we should not allow our automobiles to turn us into church consumers. Even when things become difficult, we must seek to love the church as Christ loved us — we must be longsuffering, patient, and sacrificial — abilities that only come from the grace of the gospel and the work of the Holy Spirit. Only when a church ceases to bear one of its three marks (the right preaching of the word, the right administration of the sacraments, and the right administration of discipline) should we seriously consider leaving. Irreconcilable differences may be a legal reason cited for divorce, albeit unbiblical, but it should definitely not characterize our own conduct towards the church. Just because we can drive away does not mean that we should.

FOUR

The Book

IN THE SCOPE of recorded history's roughly 5000 years, the invention of the book probably rarely crosses the mind as a technological advancement. In the minds of many, books are antiquated and now displaced by screens. Google is now attempting to scan all of the world's books, which means you can download thousands of books and store them on your computer. Who needs a physical library that takes up space, accumulates dust, and is passive. That is, when you read a book it cannot do very much in comparison with e-books. With an e-reader you can search the text, look-up words, perhaps even have your device read the book to you while you are driving in the car. The book looks somewhat dumb and mute in comparison to the 'smart' books that now seemingly dominate the cultural landscape. But with any technological advancement, there are always benefits and drawbacks. Books and e-books have great benefits, but what drawbacks are there and in what way does this impact the Christian life? In order to understand both the upside and downside of books and e-books, we need to briefly rehearse the history of the book and how it has morphed in the digital age. How has the book positively and negatively affected the church, and correlatively we must ask the same question about e-books and the digital environment from which they emerge.

The Invention of the Book

Prior to the sixteenth century, books were quite rare and expensive. However, we must go back to earlier times in order to understand how people recorded thoughts on various forms of media. In ancient times, people used clay or wax tablets. There was a limit on how much information you could record given their bulk and fragility. Papyrus and animal skin scrolls eventually superseded clay tablets and were much more suited to the task of recording information. They were more portable and writers could record an exponentially greater amount of words. But these scrolls were fragile and susceptible to the elements; they were also expensive which meant that the average person rarely owned one. Codices eventually replaced scrolls and became the first form of what we now call a book. Codices were made out of parchment or papyrus and sewn together to form a book. But once again, codices were uncommon, expensive, and typically only found in monastic libraries and churches. Ordinary people did not own codices due to these factors, so how did they manage?

On the one hand, a large percentage of the world's population was illiterate — if books were not easily accessible, then the average person had little reason to learn how to read. But nobles, monastics, and merchants had access to books and thus learned how to read, but this did not mean that they always acquired large libraries. If you were wealthy, then you could own a large collection of books. But for the average monk, owning books — or for that matter, any material possession — was not the normal practice. Nevertheless, monks took notes on temporary writing surfaces, such as wax tablets, whilst listening to speeches, sermons, or lectures. Once the lecture concluded, students could transfer their notes to a more permanent and durable medium, such as a notebook.[1] Sometimes monks would write notes in the margins of the books they were reading to preserve thoughts and interact with the text. But in the Middle Ages, people began to create notebooks with passages copied from the books that they read.[2] Monks would listen to a lecture or read a book and record their notes in one notebook. Then they would often take that same information and record it in a second notebook under topical headings. This meant that the average monk might read, copy, and re-copy the same information two, three, or more times. This had the effect of enabling the notetaker to become very familiar with the material he was learning. And beyond familiarity, prior to the invention of the mass-produced book, people would commit vast quantities of information to memory. The cheapest and most efficient way to store information was in your own mind —you could recall it on a moment's notice and carry as much information as you could remember.

We might believe that memorization was very limited and thus an inefficient means of storing knowledge, but this is not true. Medieval and early modern scholars committed vast amounts of information to memory. One sixteenth-century scholar committed Homer's *Illiad* and *Odyssey* to memory in twenty-one days. Another legal scholar memorized 36,000 names in order. Biblical scholar Erasmus of Rotterdam reportedly memorized all of the lines of Horace and Terence as a child.[3] Protestant Reformer Ulrich Zwingli memorized the entire New Testament in Greek.[4] In other words, we should not measure the human capacity for memorization by our own present (in)abilities to retain information. But the invention of the moveable-type printing press impacted things in a significant way. When Johannes Gutenberg invented the technology of the printing press, relatively inexpensive mass-produced books were now a reality. The internet did not create the information highway. It was the printing press that first opened this road. With mass-produced books, naturally, note-taking and memorization habits changed. As I like to quip to my students, 'I can't remember the answer to that question, I'm sure it's written in a book somewhere!' In other words, why commit information to memory if it is recorded in a book and I can look it up? This is not to say that people stopped memorizing information with the invention of the mass-produced book, but there was now less motivation and need to do so.

Books in the Digital Age

The age of the internet is the next technological development in the information highway. The roughly hewn paths of wax and clay tablets gave way to the dirt roads of the codex. But once the printing press appeared, the dirt roads gave way to paved highways where information could hurtle at heretofore unthinkable speeds. But with the internet, paved roads became a kind of high-speed eight-lane superhighway. Information now runs at breakneck speeds. Books have shed their incarnated forms as they have been assumed into the digital cloud. Once inaccessible ancient manuscripts and rare books are now just a click away. People can now store hundreds of thousands of books on their computers and even their smartphones. They can search thousands of books in an instant and gain access to amounts of information that no one ever conceived was possible. But like the effect of the mass-produced book on human powers of memory, the digital book also brings with it a number of drawbacks.

Research has determined that digital reading may be more convenient but ultimately has a detrimental effect on reading comprehension. What many do not realize is that human beings are creatures of habit. We can either develop good or bad habits. Recent studies reveal that now, more than, ever we are using our cell phones. In 2009, the average American phone-user was sending and receiving nearly 400 texts per month, which quadrupled from 2006. The average teenager sent and received a staggering 2,272 texts per month.[5] As we read this flurry of texts, we are training our minds to pay attention to small short bursts of information and simultaneously programming our minds to be less capable of reading larger amounts of text. Cell phones have changed the way we read because people find book-length treatments of subjects too difficult to understand.[6] We are inadvertently training ourselves to have shorter attention spans. Reading material on the internet also contributes to the diminishing ability to read sustained passages in books. When reading a web page, an individual uses a different part of the brain in comparison to when reading a physical book. When reading a book, you use portions of the brain that handle language, memory, and visual processing, but they do not employ those sections that deal with decision making and problem solving. Web readers, on the other hand, use all sorts of different parts of the brain that process all kinds of information. The upside is that web surfing can help the elderly keep their minds active like when reading a crossword puzzle. But the downside is that extensive web surfing adversely affects concentrated reading ability.[7] In other words, reading the internet or too many texts on your phone can re-wire your brain to the point where you are unable to comprehend a book.

There is a second factor that complicates things when it comes to reading e-books on computer or phone screens. When you pick up your Bible, you give the text your exclusive attention. You only read what you see on the page before you. Distractions abound on our cell phones. Sure, you can open your Bible app, but what else dances across your screen? Incoming text alerts, e-mail notifications, or the latest Twitter or Facebook message? These things distract us from the task of reading our Bibles on our phones or computers. A generation ago, Neil Postman observed this trend regarding television. He labeled Billy Graham's call for the church to use television as 'the most powerful tool of communication ever devised by man' for the promotion of the gospel. He believed

Graham was guilty of 'gross technological naiveté.' Postman subscribes to the theory that the medium is just as important as the message. That is, the message's context and mode of delivery says a lot about the message itself. He observes, 'There is no way to consecrate the space in which a television show is experienced.'[8] Postman raises an insightful observation which is still relevant in the age of the smart phone.

Postman acknowledges that almost any venue can be consecrated — a group of people can transform a gymnasium into a place of worship — a common space can become sacred. But he points out that with the transformation of the space that people change their behavior and conduct: there is no idle conversation, for example. Worshipers have a certain decorum as they sit in silence listening to the sermon. 'Our conduct must be congruent with the otherworldliness of the space.' But people do not maintain this condition when they watch a religious service on television. Postman laments,

The activities in one's living room or bedroom or — God help us — one's kitchen are usually the same whether a religious program is being presented or 'The A-Team' or 'Dallas' is being presented. People carry on as usual — they

*exercise, go to the restroom, get a drink— they do whatever
they might do while watching any other show.*[9]

But it is not just our conduct, but the actual space
of the screen that is significant. 'The television screen
itself has a strong bias toward a psychology of
secularism,' writes Postman. 'The screen is so saturated
with our memories of profane events, so deeply
associated with the commercial and entertainment
worlds that it is difficult for it to be recreated as a
frame for sacred events.'[10] Think about Postman's
observation and your phone, and it is true in spades.
What other information do you consume on your
phone? Texts? E-mails? Movies? Internet gossip?
Pornography? The same cannot be said when you open
the pages of a physical Bible — a book solely dedicated
to communicating God's word. In other words, how
much has your smartphone and Bible app eroded your
absorption of God's word because it is but one of
scores of other apps that has a grip on your attention?

A People of the Book

There are, of course, many benefits of the
technological advancement of the book and e-book.
We should not ignore these benefits. For centuries,

people were unable to own a copy of God's word and now they can hold the entirety of God's revelation in the palm of their hands; they can read it from cover to cover; they can highlight verses; they can write in the margins; and bask in the glorious truths they read on the pages of holy writ. Likewise, the invention of the e-book affords missionaries the opportunity to carry entire libraries into the field; it allows theologians to gain access to ancient books and manuscripts that only a few privileged historians could once access; and it allows us to search the collected wisdom of the ages in a matter of seconds. But, for whatever advantages the book and e-book might bring, we must also be fully aware of the disadvantages so we can properly use this technology.

Gutenberg's printing press made books affordable and widely accessible, but this should not mean that we stop writing God's word on the walls of our hearts. An inexpensive copy of the Bible is definitely a blessing, but how will Christ's words abide in us unless we mediate and memorize them (John 15:7)? The Psalmist writes: 'The mouth of the righteous utters wisdom, and his tongue speaks justice.' Why? Because 'the law of his God is in his heart' (Psalm 37:30-31). Christian prisoners of war have recounted that when they were locked in solitary confinement, it was memorized Scripture that gave them hope during their imprisonment. One prisoner described joining other prisoners in trying to recall as much Scripture as they could to share with one another. One verse came to mind, 'Thy word have I hid in my heart' (Psalm 119:11), which caused him to regret not hiding more of God's word in his heart.[11] If the apostle Paul counseled the Colossians to 'let the word of Christ dwell in you richly,' then we should not let the technology of the mass-produced book diminish our memorization of Scripture but rather strengthen it (Colossians 3:16). Now that we have access to the whole Bible in an easily portable form, we should seek to memorize as much as we can. We might not memorize the whole New Testament in Greek like Zwingli did, but what if we commit smaller but significant portions of Scripture to memory? How might memorizing Scripture positively influence our lives, give us greater growth in our sanctification, and better equip us for facing the challenges in our lives?

Similarly, just because we have the ability to use e-books and Bible apps does not mean that we should make them our default medium for reading, especially when it comes to God's word. There is a lot of research that proves conclusively that reading comprehension dramatically improves with the use of a physical book in contrast to their e-versions. The superiority of print versus e-books lies in the fact that the latter exist in an ecosystem filled with distractions. How can you settle in for a long sustained reading of a passage like Psalm 119, which at numerous points exhorts us to mediate on the Lord's precepts, statutes, wondrous works, and promises, if the continued flurry of incoming information distracts us from our meditations (Psalm 119:15, 23, 27, 48, 78, 148)? Even if the flood of texts, e-mails, and tweets abates for a while, through regular habitual use of screens we have accustomed our minds to stand at the ready for the distractions and interruptions, thus preventing us from deeply meditating upon and pondering God's word. As Nicholas Carr observes, 'The shift from paper to screen doesn't just change the way we navigate a piece of writing. It also influences the degree of attention we devote to it and the depth of our immersion in it.'[12]

Along these lines, one of the best ways to foster greater attention and comprehension of the Bible is to physically make notes. I do not mean typing them into your device but writing them down with pencil and paper, perhaps even in the margins of your Bible.

Recent research has demonstrated that students who take notes by hand outperform their typing peers. A 2012 Washington University in St. Louis discovered that typing notetakers (tested immediately after class) could recall more of a lecture than their pen wielding classmates. But after 24 hours, the laptop users forgot the material they transcribed, whereas the pen-users could remember more even a week later, and had a better grasp of discussed topics. Why? The process of writing things down encoded the information more deeply in their minds. In short, writing forces you to think more than typing. Another factor is that laptop users do not process the information they hear because they essentially take a lecture transcript — they type what they hear. But pen-users cannot write as quickly and thus must process, think, and sift through what they should write. In other words, taking notes by hand forces a person to think more.[13] Taking notes while you read is akin to writing God's word on your heart.

The other benefit of using a physical Bible is the fact that you establish some intellectual and spiritual sacred space when you turn away from the continual flow of worldly information that pours through digital devices. Niccolò Machiavelli describes the way he would transition from his daily endeavors to reading:

> *When evening comes, I return home and go into my study. On the threshold I strip off my muddy, sweaty, workday clothes, and put on the robes of court and palace, and in this graver dress I enter the antique courts of the ancients and am welcomed by them, and there I taste the food that alone is mine, and for which I was born. And there I make bold to speak to them and ask the motives of their actions, and they, in their humanity, reply to me. And for the space of four hours I forget the world, remember no vexation, fear poverty no more, tremble no more at death: I pass indeed into their world.*[14]

Machiavelli recognized that reading was not a mundane thing and so he prepared his body and mind for the task of mentally engaging, dialoging, and learning from the great minds of the past. If this was Machiavelli's mindset about reading great but nevertheless ordinary works, what should characterize our Bible reading? Should we treat it like any other book, just another app on our phone, another body of text? Or do we treat it like the word of God and have a specific book dedicated for reading and listening to God's voice speak therein? Do we sit down, strip off our worldly distractions, thoughts of work, the latest tweets and texts, and dress our minds to enter God's presence? Do we still and quiet our minds so we can enter the court of the heavenly holy of holies and seek the transforming, comforting, and life-giving word of God? If only for a brief time, do we forget the world and lose ourselves in the pages of holy writ? This is not entirely impossible with an e-Bible, but it is definitely more difficult than if you use a physical Bible.

Conclusion

Every technological advancement has up- and downsides. Simply assuming that technology only has benefits is a naïve approach to life. Paul exhorted the Romans not to be conformed to the patterns of this world but to be transformed by the renewing of their minds (Rom. 12:1-2). We need to think about this exhortation with everything in life, even the very medium where we likely encounter it, namely, a book. The same is true of e-books and the computers, smart phones, and e-readers where we read them. Weigh the benefits and the drawbacks and intelligently use them both. Be aware of how books and e-books shape and mould your mind so that you can take appropriate steps to prevent technology from adversely affecting your life. Do not let technology eviscerate your mind so that you become incapable of the sustained reading of God's word. If the church is supposed to be a 'people of the book,' the Bible, then it behooves us to be intelligent and discerning with our use of technology.

FIVE

Virtual Reality and Idolatry

WHEN I WAS a child my brother and I owned an early video game system, an Atari 2600. Some of our first games did not look like much. Pong was supposed to be like tennis but was actually two lines moving up and down trying to bounce a 'ball' (a small square dot) back and forth until one of the lines missed. Oh, how the times have changed! Video game graphics have made massive leaps since the 1980s that computer technology now allows people to experience Virtual Reality (VR). There are all sorts of ways in which VR has made inroads into our lives: we can 'experience' flight without ever leaving the ground through VR headsets or you can make virtual 'friends' on-line through Facebook. Computer technology has allowed us to create virtual worlds tailored to our personal preferences, but, as with all technology, there are both drawbacks and advantages to VR.

The Brave New Virtual World

Technology expert Kevin Kelly touts the wonders of VR, which is 'a fake world that feels absolutely authentic. You can experience a hint of VR when you watch a movie in 3-D on a jumbo IMAX screen in surround sound.'[1] Kelly likens VR to Neo's world, the chief character in *The Matrix*. He runs, leaps, and battles enemies in a computerized world. This world feels totally real to him, perhaps even hyperreal — even more real than reality. Another of Kelly's examples is the 'holodeck' on the TV show, *Star Trek: the Next Generation*. Within the confines of this room, holographic projections create objects and people that are so real that they are solid to the touch. The 'holodeck' is a simulated environment where you can create any scenario you want and live it. While today's VR technology is not as advanced as the virtual worlds in this movie and TV show, they are quickly hurtling towards this direction. Kelly recounts using the latest VR technology where he donned a VR helmet and walked through a billionaire's mansion in Malibu even though he was a thousand miles away in a real estate agent's office. Virtual reality can be used for business purposes or even for fulfilling one's fantasies — you can enter a world full of unicorns. Kelly argues that VR is not about suspending belief in the real world, but about ratcheting-up belief that you are somewhere and maybe even someone else. [2]

Certainly, there are benefits to VR technology. If you need to purchase a house but your schedule cannot accommodate a trip to your new location, a virtual tour can allay your fears about purchasing a home that you have never physically toured. Pilot trainees can employ VR to learn the fundamentals of flying without spending thousands of dollars in costly flight hours. Doctors can use VR technology to conduct surgery in remote parts of the world and give patients the benefit of receiving the best medical care in the world even if they cannot physically appear in the doctor's presence. VR driving simulators can give new drivers terrific opportunities to learn how to handle road emergencies and to make them more skilled behind the wheel, and likewise, law enforcement officers can train in shoot vs. no-shoot scenarios to make them better police officers and improve public safety. Facebook allows you to keep in touch with your friends even if you are thousands of miles apart. Or, you can enjoy a VR entertainment experience that allows to you simulate something that would otherwise be impossible, such as space travel, or exploring remote parts of the world. There are certainly many upsides to VR technology, but what are the downsides?

The Real-world Dangers of a Virtual World

For every advance and conquest of nature there is a concomitant regression. We grow stronger in some areas but weaker in others. Kelly's description of VR inadvertently signals the dangers of the technology — it 'is a fake world that feels absolutely authentic.' The technology drives a wedge between your body and your mind. Kelly describes one such experience when he was in a research laboratory at Stanford University. He was wearing a VR headset and he looked around the virtual world and soon forgot he was in a research lab and believed he was standing on a wooden plank thirty meters off the ground. He was frozen with fear as his mind told him that he was suspended high above an open pit even though his body was standing on solid ground in the research lab. Kelly's fear of heights kicked in and he nervously tried to back off the plank and then decided to jump, but since he was actually in a lab rather than over a pit his body lurched to the ground, but two lab spotters caught him before he crashed onto the floor.[3] Despite the fact that it pits your body against your mind, Kelly believes that VR will allow users a greater sense of intimacy because the technology will be everywhere and people will regularly use it.[4] In fact, Kelly predicts: 'In the coming 30 years, anything that is not intensely interactive will be considered broken.'[5] In other words, VR will become so widespread and intense that reality, or the real world, will seem insufficient. This prediction raises three important questions that flesh-out the dangers of VR for the Christian life.

Trying illegitimately to close the gap between us and reality?

One of the very real dangers of VR is that it creates an environment ripe for idolatry. An idol is anything that takes the place of God in our lives. As sinners, we have the ability to turn anything into an idol; this is not merely a weakness of VR. But VR nevertheless is a ripe environment for idolatry because it encourages people illegitimately to close the gap between themselves and reality. When God first created Adam and Eve, he gave them everything in the garden, but he placed distance between the couple and the tree of knowledge. He told them, 'Of every tree of the garden you may freely eat; but of the tree of the knowledge of good and evil you shall not eat, for in the day that you eat of it you shall surely die' (Genesis 2:16-17). If Adam and Eve wanted legitimately to close the distance between themselves and the tree, they should have followed God's command and only eaten of it when he permitted them to do so. Instead, they illegitimately tried to close the distance between themselves and the tree and they disobeyed God's command, took the fruit, and ate it resulting in disastrous consequences. We should remember that the tree of knowledge was not an end unto itself but rather it was about seeking wisdom and ultimately fellowship with God. In other words, the distance was not between the couple and the tree but rather the couple and God. Would they close the distance between themselves and God in accordance with or against his command? Adam and Eve resorted to an idolatrous substitute in their effort to close the gap between themselves and God.[6]

With VR there is a strong temptation illegitimately to close the gap between us and the world. If you cannot scuba dive at the Great Barrier Reef, then close the gap and resort to VR. If you cannot fly a plane, then close the gap and use VR. These two examples seem benign unless of course we begin to resort to VR on a regular basis. What happens when we become disillusioned with reality because it does not deliver the excitement of a VR experience? What happens when God's creation appears 'broken' because it does not satisfy like the excitement-saturated VR world? Like an athlete addicted to steroids, we become incapable of enjoying reality and thus disappear into the world of VR — a world of our own making. Like celebrities who augment their bodies with plastic surgery, they take on distorted cartoonish dimensions all in the name of shaping themselves according to their own vain imaginations. We illegitimately try to close the gap between our desires and reality by fabricating an idol that displaces the gift of God's good creation. Rather than living in the world that God created, a world that heralds his invisible power, attributes, existence, and glory, we live in a virtual world that leads back to ourselves.

Are virtual friends real?

A second danger of virtual reality is that we quickly forget that it is not real. Kelly's experience in the Stanford lab rapidly tricked his mind into forgetting that he was standing on solid ground. Few of us will likely interact with high-tech VR equipment anytime soon, but the most common form of VR we regularly use is Facebook and the many virtual 'friends' that we have. Certainly, many of our virtual friends are friends in the real world, but many of them are not. Kelly notes the challenges inherent with virtual friends because it is very difficult to determine who someone truly is online. Someone may use a fake picture, or one that has been altered, to give the impression that they are much taller or thinner than they are in real life. Kelly writes: 'Someone may present himself as a lobster, but in reality he is a dreadlocked computer engineer.'[7] One of Facebook's biggest problems is that hackers and criminals create puppet accounts with imaginary friends and imaginary friends of friends. Many of us might not have fake friends on Facebook, but how real are these 'friends'?

Among your virtual friends, how accurately do their on-line images match the reality of their lives?

How often do you see pictures of when things are great versus when things are going poorly? There are a number of studies that reveal that social media leads to depression amongst users because they continually see others having great lives and wonder why their own lives fall short.[8] Can a virtual 'friend' truly be a friend in the same sense as someone in the real world? Online friends can certainly do friendly things and be supportive, but the very best friendships require the real world context, not merely a disembodied digital state. Long before the digital age, Aristotle captured the importance of friendship:

> *In poverty and in other misfortunes, men think friends are the only refuge. It helps the young, too, to keep from error; it aids older people by ministering to their needs in supplementing the activities that are failing from weakness; those in the prime of life it stimulates to noble actions — 'two going together' — for with friends means we are more able both to think and to act.*[9]

In other words, friends assist one another in living life; in the face of real-world tragedies and challenges,

friends act as supports and guides. The author of
Proverbs touches upon similar themes when he writes:
'A man of many companions may come to ruin, but
there is a friend who sticks closer than a brother'
(Proverbs 18:24). Friends stick with one another
through thick and thin whatever the circumstance. Or,
'Whoever walks with the wise becomes wise, but the
companion of fools will suffer harm' (Proverbs 13:20).
In other words, wise people make the best friends. But
Christ identifies the pinnacle of friendship when he
told his disciples: 'Greater love has no one than this,
that someone lay down his life for his friends' (John
15:13). Christ laid down his life for his friends, his
bride, the church. These different scriptural statements
on friendship point in the direction of the real, not the
virtual, world. Some might object to this conclusion
because VR did not exist when these Bible verses were
written. This is true. Nevertheless, the applicability of
these verses hinges on the fact that we live in the real,
physical world, not a virtual world.

Here, the necessity and importance of the church
takes on a vital counter-balance for the ever-
expanding borders of digital technology. In a time
when technology is trying to redefine our lives and
encourage us to disconnect from the real world so we

can create a world of our own, true real-world friendship within the context of the church becomes an anchor to keep us grounded and tethered to God's good creation and our embodied existence. One nineteenth-century Scottish Presbyterian expressed the importance of the Christian's participation in the church in the following manner:

> *According to the arrangement of God, the Christian is more of a Christian in society than alone, and more in the enjoyment of privileges of a spiritual kind when he shares them with others, than when he possesses them apart. There is an added blessing on the fellowship of believing men, which they cannot experience except in fellowship with each other; and within the bosom and communion of the Christian society there is an enlargement and augmentation of privileges, not to be enjoyed apart from it. Such, for example, is the blessing promised to 'two or three' when 'gathered together in the name of Christ,' over and above what is promised to the solitary worshipper.*[10]

In other words, Christ redeemed us to be part of a

body, a real-world physical body called the church. When Christian friends physically gather together, they enjoy spiritual blessings in ways far greater than if they are alone: the corporate reading and listening to the preached word, the reception of the physical sacraments (baptism and the Lord's Supper), and the real-world fellowship of the saints are the means by which the church cares for the physical real-world needs of its members.

Can we really divorce our minds from our bodies?

These two observations regarding idolatry and true friendship raise an important question, namely: Can we divorce our minds from our bodies? Virtual reality encourages us to turn away from the real world, disconnect the body from the mind, and engage in a virtual world that exists in the digital realm. True, the more advanced VR becomes, it will seek to engage our body, but it will never be real — it will always be simulated — a sleight of hand as the technology convinces our mind that something other than the real world is before us. We are ensouled bodies, or conversely, we are embodied souls, and thus any attempt to rend body and soul apart will cause harm.

Just as our bodies require physical sustenance, our minds require our bodies for existence. God does not merely speak to us through his written word but also through the creation, through things. A sixteenth-century confession describes God's revelation as two books, the book of nature and the book of Scripture:

> *We know God by two means: First, by the creation, preservation, and government of the universe, since that universe is before our eyes like a beautiful book in which all creatures great and small are as letters to make us ponder the invisible things of God: God's eternal power and divinity, as the apostle Paul says in Romans 1:20. [. . .] Second, God makes himself known to us more clearly by his holy and divine Word, as much as we need in this life, for God's glory and for our salvation.* [11]

God communicates to us through the physical world, although given the fall and the effects of sin on the mind, we need the corrective lenses of Scripture to read the book of nature correctly. But this does not diminish the fact that the physical world around us is a necessary and vital witness of God's existence.

The necessity and goodness of the physical world takes on special meaning when we consider the opening verses of the gospel of John: 'In the beginning was the Word, and the Word was with God, and the Word was God' (John 1:1). 'God is spirit' (John 4:24), which means he does not have a body. Nevertheless, 'the Word became flesh and dwelt among us' (John 1:14a). The incarnation has immense ramifications for how we should beware of the tendencies of VR as it tries to separate our minds from our bodies thus detaching us from the real world. The un-incarnate Son became incarnate, which means that the physical world is a good thing given his willingness to assume a human nature. This reminds us of the goodness of the creation and our embodied state, and even in the absence of Christ's presence, our savior has given to us the Lord's Supper, bread and wine — physical things in the real world that at the same time remind us of the incarnation, the goodness of the creation, and our embodied, heavenly, future eternal state.

Conclusion

Virtual reality has a place in our lives, but the moment we allow VR to disconnect us from the real world, we run into the dangers of idolatry, diminishing the true nature of friendship, and trying to rend the inseparable connection between body and mind. Important questions to ask are: Are you using VR for entertainment or utilitarian purposes, or are you using it to displace reality? Strap on a VR helmet and take a flight where only eagles soar or take a virtual tour of your next vacation spot. However, remember that VR can never be superior to reality. If we think reality is broken and VR is superior, then it is likely that we are clinging to an idol of our own making and we need to put it down, pray that Christ would deliver us from its grip, and re-engage with the good creation. Only then can we reconnect with real-world friends, and celebrate that God has made us body and soul and, through the incarnation of his Son, has redeemed us to live heavenly, embodied lives for endless ages to come.

SIX

Unfettered Access to Evil

THE INTERNET HAS BROUGHT an information revolution to the world. We now have access to an unending plethora of data. For example, Google began the project of scanning all the world's books. According to their count, in 2010 there were approximately 130 million books worldwide and, as of October 2015, they had scanned about 25 million.[1] This is an unprecedented level of access that no previous generation in world history has ever enjoyed. Beyond books, the internet has given users the ability to access all sorts of services and products, whether hotels (Airbnb), taxis (Uber), tool services (TechShop), clothing (Stich Fix), toys (Nerd Block), or newly budding food services. We can make similar observations about shopping (Amazon) or the new types of digital content which we can now access such as streaming movies, downloading books, or even buying cars and houses.[2] As noted technology expert Kevin Kelly observes, the internet 'brings consumers closer to the producer,' what he describes as 'accessing.'[3] I have personally enjoyed the conveniences that the internet provides through this seemingly unrestricted access to a myriad of products and services. I can easily book travel for business or pleasure. I can also purchase books for my next research project which can be delivered within two days of placing my order. I can even download movies for a handy portable form of entertainment on that next business trip. There are all sorts of wonderful benefits that the internet provides. But one thing that few proponents of 'accessing' factor mention is our new unfettered access to evil.

Evil and the Internet: Pornography

It used to be that if you wanted to get a hold of pornography, you had to have the courage to go into a book store or the counter at the local convenience store in order to purchase your magazine. If you wanted movies, you had to be willing to go to the seedy side of town to buy your VHS tapes or DVDs. With the advent of the internet, people no longer have to travel anywhere. From the comfort of their own homes, people can access pornographic images and movies anonymously with relative ease, whether you search for free images or purchase a membership in a pay-per-view club. Pornography is now only a mouse-click away. What many do not realize is the financial power, prevalence, and wide-spread use of digital pornography. The estimated financial size of the worldwide sex industry is just under 60 billion dollars a year with roughly 20% of that revenue originating in the United States.[4] To put this in perspective, this is roughly the same revenue that the country music industry generates per annum.[5] The invention of the home video machine in the 1980s — and now the internet in the 1990s — shifts the pornographic industry from the dark, seedy parts of downtown into homes, offices, and dorm rooms with no signs of abatement. Today, pornography thoroughly saturates our culture.[6]

Pornography is no modern phenomenon; it did not just suddenly appear along with the internet. Every culture since antiquity has produced sexually explicit materials to arouse observers and readers. What the internet does is revolutionize how easy it is to access evil in an affordable and anonymous way. As noted above, access was more difficult but now you can discretely consume pornography without others being aware of your activity. A high percentage of online pornography is free of charge and therefore affordable. Many pay-per-view sites offer free samples that satisfy the person who does not want to pay for full-access. The internet also provides a degree of anonymity, as users can easily hide their sinful habit from the view of others.[7]

There are two important observations to make about the prevalence of pornography on the internet. Firstly, many do not realize the significant influence pornography has had on the development of technology. Pornography was a significant factor, for example, in the battle between VHS and Sony's Betamax video formats in the 1980s. Betamax had better video quality but could only hold 60 minutes of footage whereas VHS tapes could hold three hours. Sony toiled over the question of whether to adapt their technology to accommodate pornographic movies — one of the chief customers for home video technology — but in the end refused to allow the industry to use the Betamax format. Sony lost the battle and VHS tapes became the dominant format. A similar trend occurred on the internet. In 2001, there were approximately 70,000 pornographic websites, whereas today, there are about 4.2 million in the US alone. At any one point in the day, there are at least 30 million unique visitors viewing pornography. Even before the technology to stream live video existed, people were transmitting pornography over the internet through ASCII. It was the pornographic industry that pioneered online payment systems. Furthermore, in a repeat of the Betamax vs. VHS battle, High Definition DVD lost out to the higher-capacity Blu-ray when the pornographic industry chose Blu-ray as their standard format.[8] The pornographic industry was also responsible for the growth in band-width capacity; as demand for streaming on-line pornography grew, so the demand for greater bandwidth grew.[9] The connections between pornography and technology are pervasive, to say the least.

Secondly, given the ubiquitous presence of pornography, it should come as no surprise that many Christians find themselves addicted to it. A recent article documents how approximately 9 out of 10 boys and 6 out of 10 girls have been exposed to pornography before the age of 18. During the Promise Keepers movement, a survey at a rally attended by thousands revealed that half of the attendees were involved in pornography, but that was two decades ago. This same article claims that 50% of professing Christian men and 20% of Christian women are addicted to porn, and sadly, the most popular day for viewing it is on Sunday.[10] But the most troubling statistics concern pornographic addiction amongst ministers. A recent online study conducted by *Christianity Today* revealed that a majority of ministerial respondents (57% of pastors and 64% of youth pastors) indicated that they struggle with, or have struggled with pornography in the past. And 21% of youth pastors and 14% of pastors admitted that they currently struggle with pornography. More than 1 in 10 youth pastors (12%) and 1 in 20 pastors (5%) say they are addicted to pornography.[11]

To move beyond the statistics, I have had to deal with this problem in my own church in several different ways. I once had to counsel a young woman who caught one of her co-workers viewing pornography on his work computer. Tragically, this man was the father of four boys and a ruling elder in a conservative Protestant church. I counseled the young woman to talk with HR about the situation and the man was subsequently fired. In another instance, I was visiting the home of a fellow pastor and asked to use his computer to check my e-mail and discovered an icon for a pornographic website on the desktop. I wanted to avoid the uncomfortable conversation about the situation but consulted with a few trusted colleagues who counseled me to talk with my colleague. I told my colleague about the situation and he later followed-up with me to tell me that the icon was on the computer because of his son. In a third instance, I had to counsel a young man who was addicted to pornography because he was fearful that it would harm his relationship with his soon-to-be wife. Given the access, affordability, and anonymity of pornography, it is not just a problem out in the world but is a cancer within the heart of the church.

Evil in the Mundane

Pornography is a destructive evil that runs rampant on the internet, and when we think of evils, it probably tops our list. But pornography is an easy target. What about more mundane forms of evil? What about the easy access to ordinary forms of evil — things that are so common that people fail to realize its fundamental wickedness or even its connections to the demonic realm? When we read the gospel accounts of Christ's ministry, one of the regular features we encounter is his interaction with demons. We read of demon possessed people, those oppressed by them, Jesus casting demons out of people, as well as Jesus speaking about them (see, e.g., Matthew 4:24, 7:22, 8:16, 12:27, 15:22, etc). Yet, living in the modern world, I suspect that most Christians do not encounter these types of demonic phenomena. Does this mean that the demonic is non-existent? The general answer to this question is, no. Demons are real even if we do not encounter them on a regular basis, or do we? I think one of the common assumptions is that that demonic activity looks demonic. If we ran into someone wearing a red cape on his way to his Church of Satan meeting where we found satanic symbols adorning the door, then we would naturally assume that we had uncovered demonic activity. While such things do exist, we should realize that the demonic can take on a far more mundane form and is rampant on the internet.

Saint Augustine once charged the politicians of Rome with corruption because they offered his countrymen the *spectacle entertainments*. In the ancient world, Rome's 'spectacle entertainments' featured in the Coliseum and amphitheaters were scattered throughout the Empire and were a part of everyday life. These spectacles included gladiator contests, animal hunts, and even mass executions. Rome presented these spectacles for entertainment purposes, amusement, and pleasure — these spectacles touted the idea that life was cheap and death and violence were an acceptable form of entertainment. Augustine actively rejected the spectacle entertainments. In his famous *City of God,* he connected the spectacle entertainments with the demonic. Augustine writes:

> *For such demons are pleased [. . .] with the frenzy of the games, with the cruelty of the amphitheater, with the violent contests of those who undertake the strife and controversy [. . .] By acting this way [pagans] offer incense to the demons with their hearts. For the deceptive spirits rejoice in seduction; they feast upon the evil customs and the notoriously vile life of those whom they have misled and entrapped.*

In contrast to the pagan appetite for frenzy, violence, and blood, Augustine believed that God never enjoys bloodlust and violence, and as such, those who worship God should reject the spectacle entertainments.

In his book *Gifts Glittering and Poisoned: Spectacle, Empire, and Metaphysics*, Chanon Ross describes the Coliseum in the following manner:

> *The Coliseum simulated the topsy-turvy existence of the demons by elevating the spectators above the death and suffering occurring on the amphitheater floor. From his privileged seat, the spectator looked down upon the mortality of the victims as if he were gazing at it all as an immortal demon. Through an objectifying gaze, he consumed the excitement and psychosexual allure of the spectacular violence. The unfolding drama of death ignited his lusts and most wicked desires; such desires were enflamed when a lion ripped a man's arm from his body or when a gladiator delivered the deathblow. By means of a consuming gaze, he experiences life as a topsy-turvy demon, immortal yet rapt in the passions of the soul.*[12]

In this description, I hope we see how the demonic

does not have to appear as a devil in a red suit with a pitchfork but can manifest itself in the mundane. In this case, the gladiatorial games and the violence of the Roman Coliseum were ordinary, mundane, everyday events, yet Christians (like Augustine) saw through the façade to identify their evil nature. This begs the question, What in our own culture looks ordinary and mundane yet, at its core, pulsates with the demonic?

Despite all of our modern pretensions to advancement and evolution, even though 1,500 years has passed since Augustine's day, our so-called 'evolved society' still lusts for blood and regularly lathers its hands in violence as a form of entertainment that appears across the world wide web. Yes, our spectacle entertainments have slick advertising and shiny wrappers, but beneath this layer of respectability, we find the demonic. How many parents buy video games for their children that glorify violence? How many people watch sporting events that are filled with gratuitous violence? How often do people search for videos on YouTube looking for bone-crunching collisions, metal-bending accidents, or violent altercations all in the name of entertainment? Scores of websites are devoted to violence and the macabre; they present evil under the guise of ordinary fun. When I was a teenager, *Faces of Death* (1978) was a film that showed numerous clips of people dying in accidents or being mauled by animals. When the film came out on VHS, people would have viewing parties. But now, with greater accessibility, you can watch the movie on-line or clips of it, some of which have as many as 1.2 million views. There are scores of such videos on YouTube.

I am not condemning all forms of on-line entertainment, nor am I saying that there can never be excitement in our use of the internet. I am saying, however, that we have to examine carefully what we are seeking to achieve through our entertainment so we are not unwittingly conformed to the patterns of this world but renewed by the transformation of our minds as we live our lives in accordance with the teaching of Scripture. We should ask ourselves: Am I looking for violence and mayhem in my internet use? Or, am I looking to admire the noblest virtues that God has given to human beings. Celebrating skill, artistry, or heroism is one thing; celebrating bloodlust and violence is another. What are we feeding our children? Are we unintentionally nourishing them on a destructive diet of violence when we let them sit in front of the big screen and watch violent cartoons, movies, or play violent video games? These are all important questions to ask so we do not give ourselves over to the demonic in the seemingly mundane things of this world.

Finding Contentment in Christ

We must realize that in the wake of the fall, the sinful world takes two things that God has created and made sacred, twists and turns them upside down so that fallen humans exchange the truth of God for a lie (Romans 1:24). These things are sexuality and life. They have turned sexuality into perversion and they celebrate death; both aspects have become perverse forms of entertainment.[13] Both are also easily accessible through the internet. How do we respond as Christians? The answer to this question lies in three areas: discernment, detachment, and contentment. Firstly, we must not think that the technology of the internet only has benefits. We must take an honest look at how we use the internet. What do we place before our eyes and ears? Ask whether your internet use aligns with Paul's instruction to the Philippians: 'Finally, brothers, whatever is true, whatever is honorable, whatever is just, whatever is pure, whatever is lovely, whatever is commendable, if there is any excellence, if there is anything worthy of praise, think about these things' (Philippians 4:8). We need not only consume Christian forms of entertainment, but we should ask whether our movies, music, or images bring out the best or worst in us. Do the images we see drive us to lust? Do the movies we watch stir noble virtues or thoughts of anger or violence? Sifting through our internet use requires thorough knowledge of God's law and a heavy dose of Christian wisdom. Discernment is not merely about following a set of rules, as important as God's law is. Rather, it requires wisdom rightly to apply God's law to the various circumstances in our lives.

Secondly, we must be prepared to detach ourselves from some aspects of our internet usage. If you look at pornography, this is clearly sinful. As Jesus taught in his Sermon on the Mount: 'But I say to you that everyone who looks at a woman with lustful intent has already committed adultery with her in his heart' (Matthew 5:28). Pornography causes us to lust and destructively re-wires our minds to the extent that it makes people incapable of the right use of sexual intimacy. The negative effects of pornography on the mind and sexual expression has been well-documented.[14] The use of pornography is both mentally, physically, and spiritually destructive, which means that we must take the necessary steps to detach ourselves from it. The same applies to the other mundane forms of evil that we might otherwise regularly imbibe. On the heels of Jesus condemning lust as adultery, he tells us: 'If your right eye causes you to sin, tear it out and throw it away. For it is better that you lose one of your members than that your whole body be thrown into hell' (Matthew 5:29).

Biblical commentators have noted that Jesus uses hyperbole here and that he does not advocate literally gouging out your eyes. Rather, he uses this rhetorical embellishment to encourage us to detach ourselves from whatever might cause us to sin. How might you detach from pornography or mundane evil? Does your smart phone give you the opportunity to sin by viewing sinful images? Get rid of your smart phone. Better to use a basic phone than to engage in sin. Let someone you trust regularly inspect your computer for illicit images and to check your search history. I often think computer passwords are a convenient and useful excuse to keep prying eyes away from our sinful computer activity. If necessary, disconnect your internet connection. In other words, cut off your access to whatever enables and encourages you to sin through the internet. However, our desire to flee from pornography or mundane evil should not be merely about flying from sin. I once met a young man who took an axe to his dashboard to hack out his radio because the music caused him to think lustful thoughts. I commented to him that I admired his dedication but that the problem was not necessarily with his radio but with his own heart. Despite his axe-work, he was still carrying around his source of lust.

This brings us to the third and final point, namely, contentment. Because we have such easy access to all sorts of evils, we can and should take the necessary steps to flee from these forms of sin. But unless we flee from sin and run to Christ, our flight is in vain. Only Christ can satisfy our restless hearts, and until we find peace and contentment in him, we will search for poor substitutes to fill the void. As the Psalmist writes: 'For he satisfies the longing soul, and the hungry soul he fills with good things' (Psalm 107:9). As one seventeenth-century pastor counseled his church: 'If you would get a contented life, do not grasp too much of the world, do not take in more of the business of the world than God calls you to.'[15] Only when we displace the sinful desires of our hearts with a godly passion for

Christ will we find peace. And despite the ease of the accessibility of evil, we will pass it by because we only want to please Christ — the temptation fails to capture our attention because there is simply no room in our hearts for it because Christ completely fills and satisfies our desires.

Conclusion

In the end, we must recognize that the internet has given us access to all sorts of benefits, but we must be even more cautious when it comes to the drawbacks. Accessibility to good and evil is a two-way street on the internet, and thus we must be ever vigilant and discerning in our use of this technology. We must hold our lives up to the bar of Scripture to ensure that they conform, and when they do not, we must be willing to detach ourselves from whatever gives us opportunity for sin. But most importantly of all, we must pray that by God's grace he would enable us to find our ultimate joy and satisfaction in Christ alone.

SEVEN

Conclusion

———————

TECHNOLOGY IS A WONDERFUL BLESSING. It is the fruit of the many gifts that God has given to humanity — intelligence, wisdom, creativity, and industry. Humans ply their God-given minds to the creation of new things that make life easier and improve the quality of life, but we must beware of the sinful attraction to try to overcome the deleterious effects of the fall through technology. The Bible describes the cursed line of Cain as those who turned to technology and invention in the wake of his exile from the covenant community. Rather than live in the simplicity of an agrarian life like Abel and Seth, Cain's descendants were nomadic herdsmen who invented musical instruments and forged instruments out of bronze and iron (Genesis

4:20-21). This is not to say that inventing things is evil — far from it. Rather, as Martin Luther comments: 'They had turned to these endeavors and were not satisfied with their simple manner of life, as were the children of Adam, because they wanted to be masters and were trying to win high praise and honor as clever men.'[1] In other words, instead of seeking shelter in God's promise of the gospel through the seed of the woman, Jesus Christ (Genesis 3:15), they sought to fill the Christ-shaped holes in their hearts with inventions and technology. When technology begins to displace our affections for God or distort our perception of the world, we no longer use it as a tool to assist us in life — we become the instrument as the technology uses us.

Screens can be a benefit to our lives. We use computers to write books, take notes, write letters, send e-mails, pay our bills, and so on. But what happens when we have difficulty putting down the screen? What happens when our use of screens has so eroded our attention span that we can no longer sufficiently concentrate to read a chapter from the Bible? We must therefore be cautious and deliberate about how and when we use our screens. Social media has many benefits that allow us to stay in touch with friends and family, but how accurately does it reflect the world? Companies use social media outlets for advertising and selling products of all kinds, which means that we must beware lest we fall prey to slick advertising that does not truly reflect the way the world is. Nothing should ever replace the face-to-face relationships that God has given us through our friends and family. Social media should augment our face-to-face communication but never displace it. Sit down with your friends, have a cup of coffee, share your joys and sorrows. Only when you connect in person with your friends, family, and church will you truly know their needs and be equipped to help and serve them.

Automobiles are a common feature in our lives that have irreversibly shaped our culture and by extension the church. While there are undoubtedly small community churches where people live within walking distance to worship and live with their fellow church members, the vast majority of people commute to church. The ability to reach churches from greater distances is definitely a blessing, but we need to be cautious about how we use our ability to drive away from one church to another. As much as our cars might be a blessing, we must always interrogate our hearts when we feel the temptation to leave a church because we can drive away. Just because we can drive away and join another church does not mean we should. Sometimes, the best thing for us is to persevere and patiently work with our church — to be the change we desire to see in our church, to struggle through a challenging trial, or pray and intercede for our church because it is weak.

The mass-produced book is another tremendous blessing. As I write, I am surrounded by shelves full of books that I regularly use to learn, study, and seek a better understanding God's word. I am grateful that I own multiple copies of the Bible. I have Bibles at work and home as well as Bibles for travel, preaching, studying, and reference. But just because I have access to these books and Bibles does not mean that I should fail to write God's word on the walls of my heart. Why memorize portions of the Bible when we can carry it in a convenient portable form? Because meditating on and memorizing God's word is one of the best ways to draw nearer to Christ. Will you find yourself at a loss for words when your smart phone Bible app or Bible are not within arm's reach and nevertheless still be able to console a friend in a time of need, encourage a child during a trial, or minister to your own soul when doubt rains all around?

Virtual reality offers many benefits to scores of people, such as when police officers train in shoot vs. do not shoot scenarios to improve public safety. It is also fun to visit other places in the world through virtual reality. I recently toured a school where students were able to don VR headsets and tour parts of the world that they were studying. But if we use VR to the point where God's good and beautiful creation appears to be broken and lackluster, we have to ask whether we have created an idol — a world to displace and supplant God's handiwork. We must ask similar questions regarding our use of the internet. I love the fact that I have access to all sorts of unique stores around the world that sell products you just cannot get locally. I have bought a black walnut writing box from carpenters in Turkey, aluminium turned-pens that take a standard G2 refill from a craftsman in Arizona, and a white bow tie from a clothier in Norway. Buying such things twenty years ago was much more difficult. But this unfettered access to 'things' has the down side of unrestricted access to evil. Now death as entertainment, pornography, hatred, and idolatry, evils of all sorts, are a few mouse clicks away. I shudder to think of how many people, even Christians, engage in untold wickedness in the privacy of their homes whilst giving people the impression that all is well.

In each of these cases, what lies at the heart of the problematic use of technology is a lack of contentment in Christ. Like the line of Cain, we use technology as a slick and shiny, but nevertheless poor, substitute for God. Rather than drawing near to Christ, we fill our hearts and lives with our screens and the evil things we can find by browsing the internet. Instead of resting and being content with God's all-wise providence and remaining at the church where we presently worship, we hop in the car and drive away. We act more like church consumers rather than church members. Instead of rejoicing in the good, beautiful, and amazing world that God has given us, we seek to build a world of our own and replace the creation that points back to God and testifies of his glory. We revel in the virtual world that points back to our own idolatrous hearts. We fail to draw nigh to Christ through his word because we deem memorization of Scripture as unnecessary and superfluous. In blunt terms, we find less of a need to know God very well and allow his word to dwell outside of us in our Bibles or smart phones. In each of these cases, a lack of contentment in Christ lies at the heart of the misuse of technology.

When Christ fills our hearts, all of the other seemingly attractive things seem less interesting, attractive, and appealing. We can use technology like the tool it was intended to be, not as a poor substitute for Christ or something to draw us away from him. The Bible is replete with the theme of contentment in Christ. We must recognize that only by clinging to Christ do we find the life-giving source for our growth in grace: 'Abide in me, and I in you. As the branch cannot bear fruit by itself, unless it abides in the vine, neither can you, unless you abide in me' (John 15:4). Only when we feed on Christ, the manna from heaven, will we look at the world and everything that it holds out with contentment and peace within our hearts rather than a voracious hunger looking for something to fill the void. We feed on Christ through reading the word, meditating upon it, listening to it preached, and partaking of the visible word, namely, baptism and the Lord's Supper. A steady diet of God's word in our life will enable us to find contentment and peace in him. We can and must draw near to Christ through prayer — the arena in which we draw power from the Spirit's intercession to turn away and rid our lives of idols and grow in Christ. Through these means, we can tune our hearts and minds to be ready to identify anything that might turn us away from Christ. We thus do not need to live in fear of the world around us or the technology we use. Rather, by being firmly affixed to Christ, we can use God's good gifts as he intended them to be used and not allow them to lead us away from him. Therefore, do not be conformed to the patterns of the world and the technologies we use but be transformed according to the renewing of your minds by drawing near to Christ through his appointed means: word, sacrament, and prayer.

Notes

1. Screens: The New American Idol?

1. Orianna Fielding, *The Essential Digital Detox Plan: How To Achieve Balance in a Digital World* (London: SevenOaks Books, 2017), 7.
2. Kevin Kelly, *The Inevitable: Understanding the 12 Technological Forces That Will Shape Our Future* (New York: Viking Press, 2016), 85-108.
3. Kelly, *The Inevitable*, 106-08.
4. Ray Bradbury, *Fahrenheit 451* (1953; New York: Simon & Schuster, 2013).
5. Bradbury, *Fahrenheit 451*, 80.
6. See, e.g., Jean M. Twenge, *iGen: Why Today's Super-Connected Kids Are Growing Up Less Rebellious, More Tolerant, Less Happy— and Completely Unprepared for Adulthood* (New York: Atria Books, 2017), 93-118; Maggie Jackson, *Distracted: The Erosion of Attention and the Coming Dark Age* (Amhurst, NY: Prometheus Books, 2009).
7. Adam Alter, *Irresistible: The Rise of Addictive Technology and the Business of Keeping Us Hooked* (New York: Penguin Press, 2017), 1-2.
8. Alter, *Irresistible*, 2.
9. Fielding, *The Essential Digital Detox Plan*, 77.
10. William Powers, *Hamlet's BlackBerry: Building a Good Life in the Digital Age* (New York: Harper Collins, 2010), 227.
11. Kelly, *The Inevitable*, 11.

12. St. Augustine, *Confessions*, trans. Henry Chadwick (Oxford: Oxford University Press, 1991), I.i.1 (p. 3).

2. Social Media: Whose Agenda?

1. Christian Rudder, *Dataclysm: Who We Are When We Think No One's Looking* (New York: Crown Publishers, 2014), 20.

2. C. S. Lewis, *The Abolition of Man: How Education Develops Man's Sense of Morality* (New York: MacMillan Books, 1955), 71.

3. What follows comes from https://www.businessinsider.com/how-facebook-makes-money-according-to-mark-zuckerberg-2018-4 accessed 07 September 2018.

4. https://www.investopedia.com/ask/answers/120114/how-does-facebook-fb-make-money.asp accessed 07 September 2018.

5. Neil Postman, *Amusing Ourselves to Death: Public Discourse in the Age of Show Business* (New York: Penguin Books, 1986).

6. Postman, *Amusing Ourselves to Death*, 104-05.

7. Kevin Kelly, *The Inevitable: Understanding the 12 Technological Forces That Will Shape Our Future* (New York: Viking Press, 2016), 170.

8. Rudder, *Dataclysm*, 214.

9. Dietrich Bonhoeffer, *Life Together: The Classic Exploration of Christian in Community* (San Francisco: HarperOne, 2009), 77-78.

10. Bonhoeffer, *Life Together*, 27-28.

11. Bonhoeffer, *Life Together*, 28.

12. Bonhoeffer, *Life Together*, 22.

13. Martin Luther, as cited in H. S. Wilson, 'Luther on Preaching as God Speaking,' *Lutheran Quarterly* XIX (2005): 63-76, esp. 63.

14. Second Helvetic Confession, 1.4, in Jaroslav Pelikan and Valerie Hotchkiss, eds., *Creeds and Confessions of Faith in the*

Christian Tradition, vol. 2 (New Haven, CT: Yale University Press, 2003), 460.

15. Bonhoeffer, *Life Together*, 99.
16. J. Gresham Machen, *Christianity and Liberalism* (1923; Grand Rapids: Eerdmans, 1999), 180.

3. The Automobile

1. Frances Gies and Joseph Gies, *Life in a Medieval Village* (New York: Harper Perennial, 2016), 155.
2. Gies and Gies, *Life in a Medieval Village*, 162.
3. Gies and Gies, *Life in a Medieval City*, 136.
4. Scott M. Manetsch, *Calvin's Company of Pastors: Pastoral Care and the Emerging Reformed Church, 1536-1609* (Oxford: Oxford University Press, 2013), 182-220.
5. Peter J. Ling, *America and the Automobile: Technology, Reform, and Social Change, 1893-1923* (Manchester: Manchester University Press, 1990), 18.
6. Clarence Darrow, "The Automobile," in *The Twenties in Contemporary Commentary* accessed at http://americainclass.org/sources/becomingmodern/machine/text3/colcommentaryauto.pdf on 3 October 2018.
7. Warren H. Wilson, "What the Automobile Has Done To and For the Country Church," *The Annals of the American Academy of Political and Social Science* 116 (1924): 83-86, esp. 83.
8. Wilson, "Automobile," 83.
9. Wilson, "Automobile," 85.
10. Ling, *American and the Automobile*, 19.
11. Wilson, "Automobile," 84.
12. *The Book of Church Order of the Orthodox Presbyterian Church* (Willow Grove, PA: The Committee on Christian Education of the OPC, 2015), 135.

4. The Book

1. Ann M. Blair, *Too Much to Know: Managing Scholarly Information Before the Modern Age* (New Haven, CT: Yale University Press, 2010), 64-65.

2. Blair, *Too Much to Know*, 68.

3. Blair, *Too Much to Know*, 75.

4. David L. Larsen, *The Company of the Preachers: A History of Biblical Preaching from the Old Testament to the Modern Era*, vol. 1 (Grand Rapids, MI: Kregel Publications, 1998), 171.

5. Nicholas Carr, *The Shallows: What the Internet Is Doing to Our Brains* (New York: W. W. Norton & Co., 2011), 86.

6. Carr, *The Shallows*, 105.

7. Carr, *The Shallows*, 122.

8. Neil Postman, *Amusing Ourselves to Death: Public Discourse in the Age of Show Business* (New York: Penguin Books, 1985), 118.

9. Postman, *Amusing Ourselves*, 119.

10. Postman, *Amusing Ourselves*, 119.

11. https://www.andalusiastarnews.com/2011/11/12/pow-saved-by-his-memories-of-scripture-church/ accessed 11 Oct 2018.

12. Carr, *The Shallows*, 90.

13. Robert Lee Hotz, "Can Handwriting Make You Smarter? Students who take notes by hand outperform students who type, and more type these days, new studies show," *Wall Street Journal* 4 April 2016 at https://www.wsj.com/articles/can-handwriting-make-you-smarter-1459784659 accessed 12 Oct 2018.

14. Niccolò Machiavelli, "The Letter to Vettori," in *The Discourses* (New York: Penguin Books, 1998), 69.

5. Virtual Reality and Idolatry

1. Kevin Kelly, *The Inevitable: Understanding the 12 Technological Forces That Will Shape Our Future* (New York: Viking Press, 2016), 211.
2. Kelly, *The Inevitable*, 211-12.
3. Kelly, *The Inevitable*, 213.
4. Kelly, *The Inevitable*, 226.
5. Kelly, *The Inevitable*, 236.
6. On these themes, see Jean-Luc Marion, *The Idol and Distance: Five Studies* (New York: Fordham Press, 2001).
7. Kelly, *The Inevitable*, 235.
8. Jean M. Twenge, *iGen: Why Today's Super-Connected Kids Are Growing Up Less Rebellious, More Tolerant, Less Happy—and Completely Unprepared for Adulthood* (New York: Atria Books, 2017), 99-13.
9. Aristotle, *Nicomachean Ethics*, VIII.i.1155a, in *The Basic Works of Aristotle*, ed. Richard McKeon (New York: Random House, 1941), 1058.
10. James Bannerman, *The Church of Christ: A Treatise on the Nature, Powers, Ordinances, Discipline, and Government of the Christian Church*, vol. 1 (Edinburgh: T & T Clark, 1868), 91.
11. Belgic Confession, art. II, in Jaroslav Pelikan and Valerie Hotchkiss, eds. *Creeds and Confessions of Faith in the Christian Tradition*, vol. 2 (New Haven, CT: Yale University Press, 2003).

6. Unfettered Access to Evil

1. https://en.wikipedia.org/wiki/Google_Books accessed 8 Nov 2018.
2. Kevin Kelly, *The Inevitable: Understanding the 12 Technological*

Forces that Will Shape Our Future (New York: Viking Press, 2016), 112-14.

3. Kelly, *The Inevitable*, 113.

4. William M. Struthers, *Wired for Intimacy: How Pornography Hijacks the Male Brain* (Downers Grove, IN: IVP Academic, 2009), 20.

5. https://www.statista.com/topics/1639/music/ accessed 8 Nov 2018.

6. Struthers, *Wired for Intimacy*, 21.

7. Struthers, *Wired for Intimacy*, 34-35.

8. https://www.thrillist.com/vice/how-porn-influenced-technology-8-ways-porn-influenced-tech-supercompressor-com# accessed 8 Nov 2018.

9. https://www.businessinsider.com/how-porn-drives-innovation-in-tech-2013-7 accessed 8 Nov 2018.

10. http://www.expastors.com/how-many-pastors-are-addicted-to-porn-the-stats-are-surprising/ accessed 8 Nov 2018.

11. https://www.christianitytoday.com/news/2016/january/how-pastors-struggle-porn-phenomenon-josh-mcdowell-barna.html accessed 8 Nov 2018.

12. Chanon Ross, *Gifts Glittering and Poisoned: Spectacle, Empire, and Metaphysics* (Eugene, OR: Cascade, 2014), 59.

13. I owe this observation to my colleague, Julius Kim.

14. See, e.g., Struthers, *Wired For Intimacy*, 41-114.

15. Jeremiah Burroughs, *The Rare Jewel of Christian Contentment* (London: W. Bentley, 1651), 132.

7. Conclusion

1. Martin Luther, *Lectures on Genesis: Chapters 1-5*, Luther's Works, vol. 1, ed. Jaroslav Pelikan (St. Louis, MO: Concordia Publishing House, 1958), 318.